Conversations with Von Karajan

Conversations
with
Von Karajan

Richard Osborne

A Cornelia & Michael Bessie Book

1817

Harper & Row, Publishers, New York
Grand Rapids, Philadelphia, St. Louis, San Francisco
London, Singapore, Sydney, Tokyo, Toronto

Contents

List of Illustrations

PHOTOGRAPHIC CREDITS: Siegfried Lauterwasser, Überlingen 36, 47,
58 top, 58 bottom, 64, 81, 87, 95, 104, 116, 133, 140, 153; Photo Ellinger,
Salzburg 78; Reinhard Friedrich, Berlin 122; Gamma/Kurita, Paris 57;
Roger Hauert, Geneva *frontispiece*, 84; Godfrey MacDomnic, London 62,
109; E. Piccagliani, Milan 72, 74; Photo Schaffler, Salzburg 138;
Arthur F. Umboh, Hamburg 127.

Preface

HERBERT VON KARAJAN died at his home near Salzburg on 16 July 1989. Just six weeks earlier I had spent two days with him in that same house finalizing the text of this book of conversations.

Perhaps his resignation from his life-conductorship of the Berlin Philharmonic the previous April had left him with an undercurrent of reflective melancholy, but outwardly he was in good spirits, as full of off-the-record gossip and on-the-record thoughts and reminiscences as he had often been since I first met him in 1977.

Though the timing of the Berlin resignation had come as a surprise, those close to Von Karajan had guessed for some time that something would eventually have to give. His schedules in his final winter were unusually gruelling for a man in his 81st year: concerts, recordings, a European tour with the Berlin Philharmonic, his first-ever recording of Verdi's *Un ballo in maschera*, a trip to New York in February with the Vienna Philharmonic, on top of hours of film-editing for his cherished CD video project. In the end, it proved too much.

He read the typescript of the present book with the eye of a trained proofreader, though he asked for very few changes: none at all in the introductory essay and footnotes and only a handful of changes of emphasis and phrasing in the conversations themselves. He talked freely about his leaving Berlin but wanted nothing set down so close to the final break. Ever a patient man, Von Karajan always liked to get a proper perspective on things. In any case, he was too wordly-wise to see the break in purely personal terms. After 60 years in the profession he had witnessed such events at other times and in other places, though I think he was saddened by the extent of the disruption to working relationships within some of the great European and American orchestras in recent years.

The conversations that are recorded here are based on formal interviews and private conversations that I had with Von Karajan, first of all in Salzburg and Berlin in May and December 1977, and then later, and most substantially, on three visits to Salzburg and Berlin between March 1988 and June 1989. Extracts from the earliest conversations, published in the British magazine *Gramophone*, had excited a good deal of interest. The idea that they might be extended and published in more permanent form came from Oxford University Press. In 1978, Von Karajan had received an Honorary Doctorate from Oxford University and on an unforgettable evening in May 1981, he had brought members of the Berlin Philharmonic to the Sheldonian Theatre in Oxford as a token of his regard for the university. The programme consisted of Bach's

Brandenburg Concerto No. 2, Mozart's Violin Concerto No. 3 in G major with Anne-Sophie Mutter as soloist, and Richard Strauss's *Metamorphosen*, with the artists' fees donated to local charities specializing in children's heart disease, work for autistic children, and neuroscientific research. Von Karajan was thus delighted with what he called 'the Oxford idea,' and promised further time and attention once basic filming and editing had been completed on the 45 CD videos of his main repertoire. Sony Classical will be issuing these videos from 1990 onwards.

That Von Karajan was a great conductor, master of the orchestra and in a host of areas of the music he conducted is hardly in dispute in the minds of distinguished musical colleagues or the public at large. But a career that touched so closely not only on music, but also on science, technology, and aspects of politics and a theology that has as much to do with Eastern thought as Western, needs care in the handling. One day a proper critical biography will be written, and it is encouraging that to this end the Swedish historian and expert on music-making in Germany from 1918 to 1945, Gisela Tamsen, has already spent several years researching Von Karajan's early career, in the archives of Ulm, Aachen, Berlin, Koblenz, and elsewhere.

The present volume is not a critical biography. It is, rather, musical table-talk from which I hope it will be possible to deduce an impression of Von Karajan, the man and the musician, as he was in his later years.

Musical table-talk does not necessarily preclude musical politics, though for a number of reasons it was not my intention in this book to try to engage Von Karajan in a further discussion of when, why, and where he joined the Nazi Party. In the first place, a complete impasse had been reached in 1986 with the discussion of the subject in Roger Vaughan's *Herbert von Karajan: a biographical portrait*, and in Von Karajan's own brusque re-statement of his position in a hastily assembled *Autobiography* written in collaboration with the Austrian critic Franz Endler, which was a riposte to aspects of Vaughan's book. Von Karajan had always maintained that he joined the Nazi Party in 1935 as a bureaucratic condition of his being able to hold the position of Generalmusikdirektor in Aachen. He never disguised the fact that he was intensely ambitious or, after a brief spell of unemployment following his dismissal from the Ulm Opera, potentially desperate. Indeed, he often used colourfully self-deprecatory language—'I would have killed to get the Aachen job'—to underline the extent of his ambition and desperation. Unfortunately, what Von Karajan considered to be his frank statements on the matter were countered as early as 1957 by an increasingly widely publicized theory that he had joined the Nazi Party not once as a bureaucratic necessity, but twice previously, in Salzburg and in Ulm in 1933. But, as Gisela Tamsen's researches will eventually reveal in exhaustive detail, this generally accepted theory of multiple applications by a dedicated Party follower is almost certainly a fiction based on a misreading of the evidence. In Vaughan's biography, Von Karajan is nonplussed by the documents put before him. 'They are false,' was all he could say. In fact, it was not the documents that were false but the way they were being interpreted. Sadly, he had never bothered to investigate the matter for himself, and it was only weeks before his death, when he studied in some detail Tamsen's research findings, that he recognized the trap into which he had fallen.

What are the facts? First, though Von Karajan was nominated for membership in the as yet unbanned Party in Salzburg in April, 1933, he did not collect his card, sign it, or pay his dues, though the registration itself (no. 1607525) got onto the files and crops up in many memoranda and enquiries thereafter. Secondly, he did not join the Party on 1 May, 1933 despite *prima facie* evidence to the contrary. In the first place, the membership number 3430914 is too high to belong to that date. The highest number issued before the freeze on membership which lasted from May 1933 to March 1937 was 3262698. However, during the freeze, various state functionaries, diplomats and others were issued cards bearing an NG, or *Nachgereichte*, designation. These cards were, by convention, backdated to the start of the freeze: 1 May, 1933. Von Karajan's Aachen membership was an NG card, and its number accords with batches issued in 1935, the year Von Karajan had always identified as the one in which he was asked to join the Party.

Unhappily, the *prima facie* evidence was widely used against Von Karajan during his lifetime. Some of it was no doubt used in good faith, but there was also a destructive element at work. As the tenor Jon Vickers observed some years ago: 'When a man stands as high as Von Karajan and sets such a standard, when his grasp and his ability and his mind are so great, he cannot help but produce enemies. It is one of the sad things about the heart of mankind. The jealousy and envy this man is a victim of absolutely horrify me, for he is a great, great human being.' As an old man with a Nazi past it was perhaps inevitable that he should remain a focus for campaigners who understandably wish to sustain in the public consciousness a living awareness of the atrocities of the

Holocaust. But in the end, many of the campaigns against him became crazily, even cruelly exaggerated.

Nor was he spared calumny in the obituary notices and profiles that were run in the newspapers and on radio and TV after his death. In November 1989, a California-based classical music programme ran an hour-long biographical assessment that ended by explicitly linking Von Karajan with the Holocaust. Given the facts on which the presenter appeared to be working, this might have been plausible; but, again, many of the facts stood truth on its head. A fairly typical misrepresentation was the statement: 'Nor was Von Karajan a casual National Socialist. When he discovered that his second wife was partly Jewish, he promptly divorced her, in 1942.' In fact, Von Karajan *married* the partly Jewish Anita Gütermann (her grandfather was Jewish) on 22 October, 1942. The marriage ended in 1958 partly because of Anita's inability to have children, though the couple remained on friendly terms until her death a few years ago. What is more, ten days after marrying Anita Gütermann, Von Karajan applied to leave the Nazi Party. The consequence was that for the remainder of the war he got work where he could. *Persona non grata* with the government and the Party machine, he stood no chance of finding any permanent position. When Karl Böhm left the Dresden Opera, Von Karajan's application was vetoed, it is said, on Hitler's explicit order.

One of the many myths surrounding Von Karajan is that he rarely gave interviews. This is not strictly true. What is true is that, with a handful of exceptions, critics and journalists often appeared to interview the public image rather than the musician and the private man. In my introductory essay, I discuss some of the issues that are raised by Von Karajan's remarkable career and note how even competent and reasonably informed people have interviewed Von Karajan and written about him in ways that seem to wish to confirm preconceptions rather than elicit insights. It is perhaps something of an irony that a great musician is not always listened to with the kind of attention his work merits; but Von Karajan, a practical man as well as a patient one, had probably always known that. In 1977, he told me he was drafting a book on conductors and conducting. Naturally, I did not want to pre-empt his material in advance of publication, but when I mentioned this, he shook his head: 'It doesn't matter. You say a thing once and no one listens. Perhaps if you say it twenty times. . . .'

Von Karajan's capacity for long-term planning, not only of a performance he was conducting but also of a career that sought out always the best possible conditions for music-making, was one of his most remarkable qualities. At times, perhaps, it made it difficult to tempt him to cast his mind back over those sixty or more years of European music-making of which he had such an encyclopaedic and still accurate knowledge; but these conversations do, I hope, strike a balance between recollection and anticipation, whilst at the same time providing many permanently interesting insights into the craft of conducting as Von Karajan saw it.

He spoke very good English—'selectively articulate' was how Walter Legge once described it—dating back to three months he spent in England as a boy of 14 in 1922; but where a point can be clarified or the phrasing improved, I have not hesitated to do it.

In preparing these conversations, I have been grateful to the logistical help I have had over the years from a number of people, in particular, Dr Uli Märkle of Télémondial, Mrs Lore Salzburger, Mrs Antje Henneking of Deutsche Grammophon in Hamburg, Siegfried Lauterwasser, guardian of the vast Von Karajan photographic archive, and *Gramophone* magazine in London. My task was also made easier and more pleasant by the hospitality and help that was always offered by Herbert and Eliette Von Karajan and their staff at their home outside Salzburg. It was the kind of unpretentious country retreat that any Englishman is bound to envy. There was Eliette Von Karajan's garden, where the only exotica were three llamas and a charming old donkey that once appeared in *Carmen*. It was always a pleasure to talk to Von Karajan away from the razzmatazz of his working life in this handsome farmhouse set in a huge meadow ringed by hills and coniferous woods. Upstairs he was making a gallery for his wife's paintings, but downstairs everything was set out with an almost Cistercian simplicity. In June, great pots of flowers stood around the sitting-room on the scrubbed pine floor. With views across the meadow to the foot of the looming Untersberg there was no need for glamour or glitz. Von Karajan probably had everything; but in his day-to-day life he demanded very little.

As for Von Karajan himself, I was often asked what it was like to be with him. Here I imagine my impressions were not significantly different from those who knew him personally rather than through the pages of newspapers. Scores of singers and instrumentalists are in awe of the care and concern he showed for their lives and careers. Rather different, it must be said, from the small band of musicians, mainly orchestral players, whose rebarbative memoirs occasionally appear in print. Some years ago, my colleague on *Gramophone*, the critic and distinguished authority on Scandinavian music Robert Layton, visited Von Karajan in Berlin to discuss with him the music of Sibelius. Afterwards, he wrote: 'The dominant impression I am left with after this encounter is rather different from the popular image of the glossy superstar; he is completely direct and unaffected and wholly dedicated to the truth as he sees it.'

Talking to Von Karajan over many hours, it was impossible not to feel a mixture of fascination, respect, and, in the end, great affection. He was one of the most remarkable men of our age and if these reflections and conversations help us better to understand his ideals and achievements, they will have served their turn.

Richard Osborne
December 1989

Von Karajan:
Profile of a Musician

HANS SACHS   Mein Freund! In holder Jugendzeit,
wenn uns von mächt'gen Trieben
zum sel'gen ersten Lieben
die Brust sich schwellet hoch und weit,
ein schönes Lied zu singen
mocht' vielen da gelingen:
der Lenz, der sang für sie.
Kam Sommer, Herbst und Winterzeit,
viel Not und Sorg' im Leben,
manch' ehlich Glück daneben,
Kindtauf', Geschäfte, Zwist und Streit:
denen's dann noch will gelingen
ein schönes Lied zu singen,
seht, Meister nennt man die!

RICHARD WAGNER, *Die Meistersinger*, Act III

Von Karajan:
Profile of a Musician

AS our century draws towards its close, the lives of the men and
women of distinction whose careers have spanned its course take
on a special significance and interest. Herbert von Karajan would
probably have been a phenomenon in any age—musical talent of
this order, high intelligence, and such singleness of purpose rarely
go unregistered—but the twentieth-century context has made the
career an unusually fascinating one, even if it has not always been
very well understood by the apprentice biographers or the
journalists who find Karajan such an irresistible source of copy.

It has, of course, been a problem with star conductors going
back to the time of Nikisch that the conductor can come to seem
more charismatic than the music he is conducting. Not that this
need worry us unduly when we consider the excitement, the sense
of occasion, that these great musicians generate. Leonard Bernstein
once said that every Koussevitsky concert was 'a gala occasion'.
This is no bad thing. And it is no bad thing that Karajan, whose
concerts have been gala occasions now for the best part of forty
years, also sold around one hundred million records since he began
recording in earnest in 1946. There have been attempts to depict
this extraordinary achievement as a form of musical consumerism.
Robert Chesterman implied as much in a CBC radio interview with
Karajan some years ago. But the musical public is not as gullible as
some critics would have us believe. There can be little doubt that it
was the professionalism of Karajan's music-making—revered by
fellow musicians—allied to a range of truly outstanding
performances spread across a vast repertoire that had generated this
success.

Unfortunately, it is a success-story that put Karajan on a
distant pedestal in an age when politically the authoritarianism that
is part and parcel of the conductor's craft has become more than
usually suspect. This, in turn, has allowed writers and critics to
create an image of Karajan, as a man and a musician, that is
considerably removed from reality, distorting his aims and ideals
and to some extent deflecting attention away from his real historical
significance. It is a distortion that is exaggerated, in Karajan's case,
by a range of assumptions about musical interpretation and such
things as the so-called cult of perfectionism, as well as assumptions
about the relationships between music and technology, and music

and politics, that often have little factual or intellectual credibility.

At almost every level, attitudes to Karajan have been riddled with paradox and inconsistency. Since what was, in fact, a remarkably brief reign as the seeming Generalmusikdirektor of Europe (in the late 1950s Karajan held important posts simultaneously in Vienna, Berlin, Salzburg, Milan, and London), he was to some extent suspect in English-speaking countries, where there is a naturally healthy distrust of cultural super-heroes, of the idea of the conductor as *Übermensch*. Karajan the hard-working apprentice conductor, swabbing down the stage in Ulm or moving the instruments to the rehearsal hall in a wheelbarrow, is more to English taste. That, and Karajan the survivor, the man stricken with illness who none the less appeared against all the odds to conduct a musically towering, spiritually searching account of Brahms's First Symphony, as he did in London, to great and deep-felt acclaim, in the autumn of 1988. The point was well made some years ago by Hugh Maguire, a veteran of the English orchestral scene and an evident admirer of Karajan, when he said: 'He is too strong, too powerful, too rich—too much outside the general run. I haven't worked with him, alas, for twenty-five years.'[1] The sociological point is well made but it is the parenthetical 'alas' that registers the musician's feeling.

The remoteness of the man of power is something people who encountered Karajan often claimed to have found. When Christian Steiner took some much-discussed photographic portraits of Karajan in 1972,[2] he reported on the apparent remoteness and introspection of the subject. Since Karajan had a love-hate relationship with the camera, loathing its intrusions into music-making in the concert hall and uneasy with formal portraits, Steiner's observations have to be seen in their context, though it is undoubtedly the case that there was a quality of coolness and detachment about Karajan that shaped some of his music-making and made him, among other things, so formidable an interpreter of Sibelius and late Mahler. On the other hand, anyone who knew

1   André Previn (ed.), *Orchestra* (London, 1979), 180.
2   *Opera People* (London, 1982), 87–9, 111.

Karajan at all well is likely to tell of a man of great personal charm, direct and unaffected, with an amusingly sardonic wit. The last quality is interesting because it has sometimes been suggested that his music-making lacks humour, one of those generalizing statements that, typically, posits a judgement without bothering to examine the evidence. Since there was never anything at all gratuitously coarse or vulgar about Karajan's music-making, it is true that he never attempted to graft on to a score like Verdi's *Falstaff* additional jokes or belly-laughs. Though he was, by all accounts, enthusiastic about Decca's idea for the party-turns in their famous 1960 recording of *Die Fledermaus*, there was never any question of the operetta itself being subject to vulgar comic hype. Occasionally, when Karajan has conducted an Offenbach overture with unusual verve and power, one is reminded that Bismarck was one of the Frenchman's greatest admirers; but inasmuch as Karajan's own personality seeps into his conducting of comic music, it is a certain mordancy of spirit that shines through. The black comedy of the gallows scene in Verdi's *Un ballo in maschera* is very Verdian and also very Karajanesque; and though Karajan often made out the critics in Strauss's *Ein Heldenleben* to be a nicer bunch than they probably are, I have yet to hear a more vitriolically gossipy performance of the 'Tritsch-Tratsch' Polka than the one Karajan conducted with the Philharmonia Orchestra in one of his last recordings with them in September 1960.

The fact that Karajan was a man of considerable good humour, with a fund of musical anecdotes and a talent for musical mimicry, does not obscure the existence of that more private self that Steiner claims to have glimpsed and which was also evident in Karajan's long-standing preoccupation with skiing, flying, and sailing, activities not of some rich playboy, but of a person who since childhood had been uneasy with gregariousness and the urban life. The desire to be alone with nature, which Karajan's elder brother took to the point of eccentricity, was there in Karajan too; an impulse, at once delighted and dispassionate, to slough off mundane things. Karajan would agree with the poet Hardy, 'Mind-chains do not clank when one's next neighbour is the sky.'

Schoenberg described the Mahler of the Ninth Symphony as a

man 'at home with spiritual coolness', which is something that
Karajan, as an interpreter of Mahler's music, undoubtedly
understood. It is there, too, in his fastidiously beautiful and
penetrating conducting of Puccini's *Madama Butterfly* for Callas in
their 1955 Milan recording. And it is there in his conducting of
Debussy's *Prélude à l'après-midi d'un faune*, which the English
Wagnerian Reginald Goodall once singled out as conducting that
managed by some unique alchemy simultaneously to catch a sense
of fire and ice, sultry heat and marble calm.

In 1956, the French critic Bernard Gavoty published a
monograph on Karajan that was much preoccupied with Karajan's
temperament and musicianship at a time when he was being
increasingly regarded more as an ambitious virtuoso superstar than
as a totally dedicated musician. At the heart of the essay is a
description of Karajan conducting a Lucerne Festival performance
of Honegger's *Symphonie liturgique*. Gavoty knew Honegger and
had discussed with him this astonishing work—'a drama in three
acts, a formless prayer articulated by a world in turmoil'—which
Honegger had written in the winter of 1945–6. After describing the
symphony in richly metaphorical prose, Gavoty came to the coda,
a kind of *dona nobis pacem*, and to Karajan:

The city is dead and the stones smoke, but day breaks and the innocent
bird pipes joyously above the ruins. The little flute practises its exercise,
and then all is silent, because all is said. Whom was I speaking to? No
longer to you, Herbert von Karajan, but to the nameless crowd which
Honegger is addressing from the pinnacle of his genius. Let us calm down
now, and resume our equanimity and the scarcely broken thread of our
argument. For this chance fever which had just laid me prostrate was not
induced by Honegger alone but by you too. The greatest composer in the
world, if he lacks an interpreter to suit him, is like a man prevented from
speaking by a gag; and this evening it was you who acted as the interpreter
to untie the gag, the messenger to carry the good news. You played your
part like the great tragedian you are. Not that you were dissimulating
unfelt emotions: you were merely their translator, and you transcended
those emotions, imparting to them that furnace heat which makes a work
of genius give off light if it is brought to the desired temperature. Even as
you were ordering the march of your troops you made some of those
sudden discoveries which throw more light than a painstaking analysis. In
the finale, as the whole orchestra was pronouncing the triple supplication

'Do-na-no-bis-pa-cem', all at once a wonderful gesture escaped you: you plunged your left fist deep down as if you were setting the torch to the side of a funeral pyre. Immediately the whole orchestra burst into flame. From my seat I could see your profile. And truly it was no longer, as I had once thought, a matter of a star courting success by adopting the affectations of a prima donna, but of a man who has given himself up to a trance. You were a medium, in the full force of the word, maintaining the subtle link between the musical work and the audience. For one instant I saw you, erect on tiptoe, ruling your orchestra and transfigured by the expression of a conqueror. A Luciferian fire was consuming you—which means that at that moment you were bearing light. Thus in one moment the veil which had been preventing me from seeing you as you are had been lifted. What I had mistaken for affectation was nothing but concentration. In the act of conducting you made such inward exertions that you had not enough energy left to watch over the outward appearance. And you only seemed artificial in so far as you disregarded the customary devices of false simplicity.[3]

Karajan's response to Honegger's *Symphonie liturgique* and its near contemporary, Strauss's *Metamorphosen*, of which he made the first recording in 1947, provides specifically musical evidence of Karajan's priorities and allegiances that I have yet to see considered by those who have become so concerned to analyse and recycle often erroneous information about his alleged political sympathies before and during the Second World War.

There is no doubt that Karajan was able to observe musical power-politics at close quarters, having arrived by some malign chance in 1937–8 as a possible rival to the politically recalcitrant Furtwängler. But looked at in its full historical perspective, Karajan's career from 1929 to 1949 was as subject to trauma, disruption, and the vagaries of the times as the next man's. To read some of the *ad hominem* propagandizing directed against him in the post-war years, one might imagine Karajan was a great player in this awesome drama. In reality, he was more pawn than player, talented, hard-working, and insecurely based. Having been sacked from Ulm in 1934 for excess of talent, he survived in Aachen only until 1942. After the war, his career was interrupted by the Allies'

3 Bernard Gavoty, *Herbert von Karajan* (Geneva, 1956), 13–15.

investigative tribunals and partly blocked in Berlin, Vienna, and
Salzburg by the machinations of Furtwängler. Walter Legge once
said that Karajan was not interested in politics, except of the
musical variety, of which he was to become a consummate master.
But even this remark states only part of the truth. Despite
Karajan's meteoric ascent to positions of power and influence after
Furtwängler's death in 1954 and Böhm's dismission from Vienna
some months later, it is clear that Karajan's ultimate aim was not
power but independence: hence the contract for life with the Berlin
Philharmonic, hence the founding in 1967 of the Salzburg Easter
Festival, brilliantly engineered and financed by Karajan after his
return to influence in Salzburg and his eight-year reign at the
Vienna State Opera. Where politicians have challenged him, he has
outmanœuvred them until such time as he perceived his work to be
done; and then—Vienna 1964, Berlin 1989—he simply and quickly
stepped aside to move on to fresh projects.

Karajan had always been clear within himself what his aim in life
was. In the winter of 1945–6, when he took himself off into the
mountains on spiritual retreat, he wrote to one of the United States
Army's cultural attachés with whom he later became great friends:

Your letter was a great joy to me, a message from another human being
who approaches his work with the same seriousness as I do mine, and who
has consequently suffered as much under the insanities of our time . . .
Early this year I secluded myself up here for a life of quiet, concentrated
study and meditation, rediscovering myself in the vastness and solitude of
the mountains. I feel wonderful inside and out, it has been the most
productive period in ages, and one day I'll need my sound nerves more
than ever . . . My own plans are still totally up in the air, except that I am
sure to resume my work when the new season gets underway—and then I
am just going to make music wherever I am offered the best conditions for
it.[4]

Later, if he was not offered those conditions, he created them for
himself.

Despite all this, and more that any fully researched biography of

---

4   Quoted in Roger Vaughan, *Herbert von Karajan: A Biographical Portrait* (London, 1986),
    142–3.

Karajan would reveal, it is a curious fact that writers of influence continue to play out their own strange fantasies when writing about the fictional Herbert von Karajan, a kind of latter-day Frankenstein's monster of their own contriving. Fortunately, Karajan's career is so well documented, officially and unofficially, on gramophone recordings, it is possible to check for oneself whether the performances tally with some of the more outlandish descriptions we have of them. And yet there is here, as with so many issues surrounding Karajan's work and reputation, the wider question of the degree to which we hear what is there as opposed to what we imagine is there. Karajan is not the first conductor to be affected by this. For years it was believed that the 'fanatic' Toscanini conducted everything very fast, though it is an attested fact that his Bayreuth *Parsifal* was the slowest in the theatre's history and that his famous *Falstaff*, not to mention a good deal of his Mozart and Brahms, was unusually broad in its pacing. And at a time when Furtwängler was out of fashion in Britain and America it was not unusual to be told that he rarely managed to play two successive bars in the same tempo. With Karajan we have the mythology of the suffocatingly beautiful sound and, beyond that, the *ad hominem* fantasies briefly alluded to above. When in 1988 Deutsche Grammophon reissued on compact disc the recordings Karajan made in Berlin, Amsterdam, and Turin between 1938 and 1943, the *New York Times* published an article on music-making in wartime Germany that concluded with the speculation that in none of the recordings Karajan made at this time is there any evidence that 'the soul was troubled'.[5] As a bravura end to an unpleasantly tendentious article, it was no doubt very effective. As a critical or psychological judgement it is meaningless, since it is difficult to see how a conductor can reveal private soul-searching whilst recording the overture to *Die Fledermaus* or Beethoven's Seventh Symphony, short, that is, of transposing each piece into the minor and playing it at half speed. There is, in fact, every indication that Karajan was acutely aware of the temper of the times, though to find evidence of this we do not go to the random rag-bag of recordings he was permitted to make in the early 1940s but to what he immediately

5   Will Crutchfield, *New York Times*, 28 Aug. 1988.

turned his mind to with Legge in Vienna in 1947: Strauss's *Metamorphosen*, a recording, still, of unparalleled intensity, and the Brahms *German Requiem*, a performance (it was said to be one of Toscanini's favourite records) of unbearable directness and poignancy of utterance.

Karajan's return to music-making and recording in 1946–7 was brought about with the help of Legge and, at much the same time, the great Italian conductor Victor de Sabata, another man totally given over to music but whom the whirligig of public opinion had rightly exonerated despite extensive war work in both Italy and Germany in front of audiences of all manner of political persuasions. Karajan's first success was the 1946 Vienna Philharmonic recording of Beethoven's Eighth Symphony. Since he was barely known in Britain at the time, the review of the recording in the March 1947 issue of *Gramophone* makes no mention of Karajan himself, let alone any gratuitous remarks of the crash of boots and jingle of spurs variety. Rather, the reading is commended for its 'cordiality', its 'high musicianship', and the sense it conveys of Beethovenian power and humour.[6]

Karajan did emerge in the late 1940s, none the less, as a musician capable of both exciting and shocking settled assumptions. Another *Gramophone* critic found his Viennese recording of Beethoven's Fifth Symphony unpleasant in its ruthlessness, in marked contrast to a performance of the symphony at Karajan's début concert with the Philharmonia Orchestra in April 1948 which the reviewer remembered for its grasp of musical architecture and its remarkable intensity of feeling.

A number of reviews of Karajan's early recordings with the Philharmonia Orchestra were written by the precociously gifted Andrew Porter, a critic often quoted by the anti-Karajan lobby or adulatory biographers looking to add some grist to the mill. In fact, Porter is not only one of the longest-serving writers on Karajan, he is also one of the best-balanced. His review of Karajan's famous Philharmonia recording of Strauss's *Don Juan* and *Till Eulenspiegel*—Columbia's first LP on 33CX 1001—placed Karajan in the Toscanini and Koussevitsky tradition. With the Philharmonia wind players at their vaulting, brilliant best, it was a performance which Porter found himself preferring to the mellower and long-admired Clemens Krauss recordings, which sounded tame by comparison. Similarly with Debussy's *La Mer*; Porter found a gentler and less exciting alternative, this time the Ansermet recording, and again put Karajan in the Toscanini/Koussevitsky tradition, adding for good measure the name of Charles Münch. The review of the recording of *La Mer* is especially interesting for the debate it prompts within Porter imself, who admits to a prejudice against some Karajan performances, not before they start, but within moments of the opening, when it might be felt that—in those days—too much was being made of the music. But in the end he capitulates: 'But, oh, the fiery approach, the almost fierce care with which every string phrase, every woodwind entry, is nursed, making Karajan's a thrilling performance.'⁷ It is a debate that Porter has continued across the years. When the Berlin Philharmonic visited New York in 1982, he registered some doubts about aspects of the music-making, about an absence of cut and thrust in the articulation of some of Brahms's cross-rhythms, but went on:

The third concert, of Brahms's Third and First symphonies, revealed the new Karajan at his most lovable, for these were natural, emotional, and— let the word escape at last—profound interpretations: voyages of discovery; loving traversals of familiar, exciting ground with a fresh eye and mind, in the company of someone prepared to linger here, to exclaim there; summations towards which many of his earlier, less intimate performances of the works had led.⁸

Karajan had pitched camp with Legge and the Philharmonia in 1949 when a generous grant from the Maharaja of Mysore had stabilized the orchestra's finances and opened up the possibility, in collaboration with EMI, of extensive recording, not only of the classic repertory but of works that caught Karajan's and Legge's fancy: Balakirev's First Symphony, Roussel's Fourth Symphony, the still formidably difficult *Music for Strings, Percussion, and*

7 *Gramophone*, 31 (1954), 333.
8 Andrew Porter, *Musical Events: A Chronicle 1980–1983* (New York, 1987; London, 1988), 339.

Celesta by Bartók, and some English music, too. Karajan's 1953
recording of Vaughan Williams's *Fantasia on a Theme by Thomas
Tallis* was generally preferred to some home-grown recordings.
(Later, Karajan was to lay claim to Holst's *The Planets*, first with
his Vienna Philharmonic Decca recording, a favourite of the
composer's daughter, Imogen, and subsequently with his Berlin
recording which, with a mixture of bemusement and pride, Karajan
would tell you is one of his all-time best-selling records.)

In his autobiographical reminiscences with the Viennese critic
Franz Endler, Karajan has explained why, for all its youthful
brilliance, the Philharmonia was not an orchestra he felt he could
grow with beyond a certain point. Like most of Karajan's
judgements, it is rational and soundly based, though it will always
disappoint English music-lovers for whom the early 1950s
Philharmonia was a high-water mark in the country's orchestral
affairs, matched only by such other brief periods of glory as those
enjoyed by Beecham's LPO and Boult's BBC SO in the 1930s and
the LSO in the Monteux, Kertész, and early Previn years. Karajan's
work with the Philharmonia was both brilliant and painstaking.
And, despite some tensions, generally social rather than musical and
mostly on tours abroad, there is no doubt that his work with the
orchestra helped revolutionize the whole idea of the conductor–
orchestra relationship.

Because Karajan was a legend in his own lifetime and thus in
some ways indistinguishable from the legendary figures of the past,
it is important not to overlook the ways in which he effected a
thoroughly modern revolution in both the method and the manner
of orchestral training. It is an aspect of Karajan's work and
influence that makes him more the forebear of Simon Rattle than
the successor of Arthur Nikisch.

André Previn has described Karajan as 'the great motivator';
Ashkenazy has called him 'a great intuitive musician who
communicates as well as anyone could imagine'. He was, in fine, a
great teacher. This was evident to me the first time I attended a
Karajan rehearsal, and even more so in the first of our long
conversations. It has also been clear in his methods of training
orchestras over long periods of time. Though in the last resort any
conductor is an autocratic figure, Karajan's methods of musical

preparation tended to be practical and co-operative rather than formal or didactic. It has been said that he understood the psychology of an orchestra better than almost any other conductor. In the first place, his rehearsals were always scrupulously prepared; in the second, he generally tried to ensure that the players themselves felt that they were ahead of the game. Rehearsals, older Philharmonia players recall, never overran. However pressed they were, Karajan would always contrive to finish that little bit early. If a player was obviously off colour, Karajan would never harry him. One player has recalled:

I've always greatly respected von Karajan, simply because he treated you man to man. The first time I played with him we were doing *Don Juan*. I was a new face in the orchestra, very inexperienced, I'd never played the piece, though I'd studied it and practised my part. Well, in the beginning the strings sweep up, then there are the basses and the bass trombone, which has the phrase on the beat, and it has to be there. Von Karajan made some loose, ethereal movement which the strings understood and the first fiddle led them up the sweep. But I couldn't see or feel a downbeat at all—he just had his arms in the air, he wasn't going to beat like a bandmaster—and I missed the entry. I think most conductors would have stopped and made a song and dance. Von Karajan simply looked over, as if to say, 'I know my job, I hope you know yours. I won't say anything now, but when we come to the recapitulation you'll know what I am doing, and we'll see what you do'. When the recapitulation came, of course, I was ready and played it. He just glanced over again, as if to say OK, but not a word was spoken. Von Karajan was fine. Well, he was a real man, a real general man, he drove fast cars and flew an aeroplane as well as being a fine musician. I could get on with a man like that.[9]

With the Berlin Philharmonic Karajan was able to extend the scope of his musical preparation not just across days but across weeks and even years. In the conversations, he talks of preparing Mahler's Fifth Symphony over two years of play-throughs, rehearsals, and recording before the first concert performance in Berlin. He spoke on another occasion of the music 'resting in the mind of the players'. For some years I had had a similar experience in the teaching of literature, amazed to see colleagues attempting to

9 Previn (ed.), *Orchestra*, 161–2.

hound students, in the context of a two- or three-year course, through complex texts in a single session: today we read *King Lear*, tomorrow we discuss it, and next day you write your essays on it. Absurd as this is, it happens all the time. Karajan's methods were as commonsensical as they were revolutionary, reminding one of Confucius's puzzled enquiry, 'The way out is via the door, how is it no one will use this method?'

Seiji Ozawa, a Karajan pupil, has reported how, as a teacher, Karajan would identify a point at issue but never proffer a solution, conforming to another fine adage of teaching: 'You may take the pupil to the window but on no account should you attempt to describe the view.' To Karajan these things were second nature.

Because Karajan was a born teacher, he was always interested in young musicians. This is not always an easy course to take. It can so easily look like a stunt or be represented as a desire wilfully to shape malleable material. The risk factor is high, teachers and even parents sometimes jealously interfere, orchestras can take umbrage at being asked to work with prodigies. Karajan took all this in his stride. I vividly recall attending a rehearsal in Salzburg at Whitsuntide 1977. It was mid-afternoon and Karajan led the Berlin orchestra, more or less without break, through *Ein Heldenleben*. The Strauss completed, a young girl appeared in jeans. Karajan came down from his high conducting stool, the orchestra regrouped for a Mozart concerto, and for the rest of the afternoon the music-making was active and intense, full of a special vibrancy and good humour. The young girl was called Anne-Sophie Mutter, whom Karajan took with him to Oxford for his special thank-you concert in the Sheldonian Theatre and whose career has developed formidably since 1977.

Karajan was a man easily absorbed in what D. H. Lawrence in a famous schoolroom scene once called 'the passion of instruction'. On another occasion, after the sessions for the recording of *Der Rosenkavalier* had been completed one January afternoon in 1982, I recall him rehearsing the Vienna Philharmonic in two works by Tchaikovsky, the Sixth Symphony and the Fantasy Overture *Romeo and Juliet*. It was late afternoon, the microphones had been taken away, the hall was only half lit. Karajan sat with the orchestra in something closer to a seance or seminar than a rehearsal. Occasionally, he would break the spell with a droll reminiscence, but for the most part he worked patiently and quietly, first on the symphony and then on the overture, where the work was even more quiet and concentrated, the string recitatives fashioned with a care most conductors would reserve only for the recitatives in the finale of Beethoven's Ninth. Afterwards he told me that one or two of the younger players in the orchestra had never played the overture before. At the time I was surprised by the information; yet in retrospect it struck me that this, above everything else, was what had meant most to him during that afternoon's work.

Karajan had always been an assiduous rehearser. In Aachen, he said, he spent sixty or seventy sessions a time simultaneously working on and training the choir in works like Bach's B minor Mass and Beethoven's *Missa Solemnis*. With the young Wilhelm Pitz as the chorus-master of the local Opera Chorus in Aachen, it must have been a formidable combination. But Karajan's assiduousness has, inevitably, been derided and criticized, the propagandists coming up, on this occasion, with the word 'perfectionism'. That the word is intended pejoratively was made clear in a 1987 BBC radio documentary on Karajan entitled 'The Price of Perfection'. In fact, Chesterman had put the charge of perfectionism in person in his CBC interview, where Karajan had suggested that the word was one used by those too idle or impatient to attend to the basic disciplines of their craft. Music, Karajan argued, has every right to be played as accurately and beautifully as possible. When Chesterman countered with the suggestion that this was all very technical and cerebral, Karajan— a courteous man who normally conducted a conversation with the calmness of a trained philosopher—retorted with the suggestion that such a view was 'misguided'. After long and careful preparation, he went on, his orchestra was able to play music with full knowledge and without fear of error. Unlike many orchestras, the Berliners, he suggested, do not play at the edge of their musical tolerance, hounded by fear, 'swallowing the notes'. They play, instead, joyfully, with a full command that allows them in performance to play, not as men chained to their scores, but as men making music with free intelligence and full imagination. It was a wonderful answer; and, indeed, it is the sight and sound of this modern miracle that Karajan worked long years to register and preserve on film.

But let us take another view of this perfectionism that Karajan is accused of, with another quotation:

Certainly, many have extolled his demonic personality, his unheard-of sense of style, the precision of his performances as well as their tonal beauty and clarity. But, for example, among other things I have heard one of his 'colleagues' say that there is no special trick to bringing off good performances when one has so many rehearsals. Certainly there is no trick to it, for the oftener one plays a thing through, the better it goes, and even the poorest conductors profit from this. But there is a trick to feeling the need for a tenth rehearsal during the ninth rehearsal because one still hears many things that can become better, *because one still knows something to say in the tenth rehearsal*. This is exactly the difference: a poor conductor often does not know what to do after the third rehearsal, he has nothing more to say, he is more easily satisfied, because he does not have the capacity for further discrimination, and because nothing in him imposes higher requirements. And this is the cause: the productive man conceives within himself a complete image of what he wishes to reproduce; the performance, like everything else that he brings forth, must not be less perfect than the image. Such re-creation is only slightly different from creation; virtually only the approach is different.[10]

A better description of Karajan's method and aim would be difficult to find, though the passage was in fact written by Schoenberg as a description of the conducting of Mahler. Since Mahler and Karajan both held the position of head of the Vienna Opera, Neville Cardus was once tempted into concocting a comparison between the two men and finding a good deal in common.[11] One should always be careful, of course, not to confuse the creative artist with the re-creative one (as Verdi once remarked,

10   Arnold Schoenberg, *Style and Idea*, ed. Leonard Stein (London, 1975), 464–5.
11   Neville Cardus, 'No Conceit: Karajan and the Vienna Philharmonic', *The Guardian*, 5 Apr. 1962. Cardus noted their obvious mastery, their distrust of the perpetual backward glance, and their capacity to give offence to the prevailing establishments and bureaucracies of the day. He might have added their preoccupation with the effective staging of musical events. Mahler's overseeing not only of the music at the Munich première of his Eighth Symphony but also of the seating, lighting, and schedules of the city trams is something Karajan would have found quite comprehensible.

that is the way to the abyss). Equally, one should perhaps guard
against the maxim that a conductor who is not also a creative writer
is somehow debarred from access to the grail of ultimate musical
understanding. Schoenberg, in his essay on Mahler, sees the
capacity to 'conceive within' oneself 'a complete image' of what one
wishes to reproduce as the crucial element.

Karajan, it seems, always had a superb baton technique. Singers
like Elisabeth Grümmer who worked with him in Aachen attest to
the fact; it has been elaborately described by Legge;[12] and Karajan's
younger colleagues remark on it still. To quote Ashkenazy again:
'He gives the orchestra very strong signals from very subtle
impulses.' Given, in addition to this, a substantial dose of what the
Germans call *Ausstrahlung*, a capacity to radiate energy, rehearsing
may seem to be *de trop*. For some great conductors it was—
Karajan, like everyone else, had a good line in Knappertsbusch
stories—but Karajan's repertory and reputation have not been built
on that premiss. As James Galway wrote after some years with the
Berlin Philharmonic, 'Karajan would never accept the standard
noise.'[13] We can hear that for ourselves in the records that have
been issued of Karajan rehearsing the late Mozart symphonies or
the Finale of Beethoven's Ninth Symphony. During the final
rehearsals for the 1962 Berlin recording of the Ninth, Karajan
discovered that for years in the Finale's 'adagio ma non troppo, ma
divoto' the Berlin violas had been annexing for themselves the top
line in a passage that is richly divided. Later, at bar seven, there is
this classic exchange:

KARAJAN. You always make here an enormous pause which isn't shown—
it's falsification of a document.
ORCHESTRA. But what about the dots [staccato marks]?
KARAJAN. They are there to get good attack so the notes are well
articulated. They have nothing to do with the length of the notes; that's a
fallacy, and let anyone who teaches this in an academy be turned out as a
misleader of the people! In time, please.

In his autobiography, *Putting the Record Straight*, John Culshaw

12 Walter Legge, *On and Off the Record*, ed. Elisabeth Schwarzkopf (London, 1982), 220–31.
13 James Galway, *An Autobiography* (London, 1978), 159.

describes Karajan working on the Card Scene in his RCA recording of Bizet's *Carmen* made in Vienna in 1962–3 with Leontyne Price as Carmen:

We had just finished the Card Trio in Act 3 with Leontyne and the two other gipsy girls in splendid voice, while Karajan's accompaniment had been an education in itself. On paper, there is almost nothing worth mentioning—just a series of slow, equally spaced string chords, which nine conductors out of ten treat with something approaching disdain. They are easy to play; they plod along, and the interest is in the voices and the text. It was evidence of Karajan's genius or magic or whatever we care to call it that he took enormous pains with these simple chords in order to get just the right degree of string tone with an appropriately dark colour. He balanced the string sections between themselves. I know that sounds very obvious and even commonplace, but it is not. Most conductors just sit down at that point and, beyond making sure that the orchestra kept up with the stage, leave the music to its own devices. What he brought to the Card Trio was what the singers also brought, which is dramatic tension; and yet its subtlety is such that it does not draw attention to itself, but simply contributes to the dramatic fabric of the whole. I do not think that a single critic noticed that it was any different from the customary 'rum-te-tum', but if one of them did he evidently didn't think it was worth a comment.[14]

The complementary element to this in Karajan's conducting has been the unusually wide distinction he made between the technique required for rehearsing and the qualities needed by a conductor in an actual performance, something he spells out in our conversations. Karajan has always been famous for his willingness to breathe with players—wind players in particular—something that many conductors neglect to do. Indeed, it is so much within Karajan's music-making faculty that he would breathe with the music even when watching a TV monitor in a video editing session. But Karajan did more than breathe with players during live music-making; he was happy to grant them what Galway called their sense of 'fantasy':

If somebody had a good fantasy . . . Karajan would give that fantasist all

14   John Culshaw, *Putting the Record Straight* (London, 1981), 335–6.

the freedom he needed because he knew that what appeals to an audience is something arising out of the immediate performance, out of something that is happening within the mind of the musician at that moment.[15]

The music critic of the London *Daily Telegraph*, Peter Stadlen, put it slightly differently when Karajan conducted Bruckner's Fifth Symphony at the Royal Festival Hall in May 1981:

Karajan's devout acceptance of what there is proved to be the Fifth Symphony's best bet, given the untold care and effort that has gone into the shaping of the minutest detail of phrasing and, indeed, colouristic effect. Hence there is nothing improvisatory about the collaboration between this conductor and his orchestra. Rather does Karajan seem to remind them at every point of what they had agreed on in countless hours of common endeavour; and his movements—chiefly of the baton-less left hand—are functional, not in the least demonic. If none the less there is no question of *déjà entendu* but a sense of compelling actuality, it is because the unique partnership appears to inspire every one of these outstanding players to feel responsible not only for his part but for the reading as a whole. I even felt this about the two trombones, who did not join the magnificent brass corps until its final chorale.[16]

The rebuilding of the Berlin orchestra was begun by Karajan in 1955 with great patience and care—he had a lifetime's contract in the process of final negotiation. Initially, he recorded comparatively little: an *Ein Heldenleben* for Deutsche Grammophon, a grand, craggy Bruckner Eighth and an exquisitely poised account of Mozart's A major Symphony, No. 29, K201 for EMI. Outside Germany, a wider public became aware of the younger, refurbished band when Karajan toured the nine Beethoven symphonies in 1961 before the integral recording for Deutsche Grammophon which pioneered the idea of the 'subscription set' in the new stereo age. Anyone who has not seen Karajan's Berliners in full cry—the CD videos will rectify this omission in the fullness of time—can at least

15 Galway, *Autobiography*, 159–60.
16 Peter Stadlen, *Daily Telegraph*, 28 May 1981. Cf. Andrew Porter's review of Karajan's Vienna Philharmonic performance of Bruckner's Eighth Symphony, Carnegie Hall, New York, February 1989: 'But one had the sense—rarely conveyed by the crack orchestras that never get a note wrong—that the players were not so much obedient, virtuoso servants of the conductor's will, as, to a man, sharers, collaborators, in an interpretation' (*New Yorker*, 20 Mar. 1989, 90–1).

catch something of the wonder of the spectacle in the piece Neville
Cardus wrote about the first of the 1961 Beethoven concerts in
London. It must be said that Cardus's review expressed the
reservation that there was, perhaps, some sameness of carriage and
accent in each of the three performances, whether it was the First
Symphony, the Seventh, or the Apollonian Fourth (a reading
Karajan later modified); but his review characteristically paints a
picture, sets the scene for the absent reader:

Herbert von Karajan and the Berlin Philharmonic packed the Royal
Festival Hall on Friday, and at the end of a Beethoven programme the
uproar of applause was quite demented. The playing throughout the
evening was truly superb, every instrumentalist bowing and blowing and
thumping as though for dear life. The violins waved and swayed like
cornstalks in the wind. The drummer, white haired, might have been a
conjuror drawing rabbits from his instrument's interior. One cello player,
at least, swept his bow with so much passion that he seemed likely to roll
off the platform. Every note had vitality, yet every note was joined to all
the others. There were no tonal lacunae, not a hiatus all night. We could
hear things in the score which usually we are obliged to seek out by eyes
reading the score. Phrase ran beautifully into phrase, viola took on from
violin, cello from viola without an obvious 'join'. The double-basses were
magnificent and capable of quite delicate shading. Woodwind choired,
perfectly blended. The violins were alternately warm and brilliant. It was
never a case of merely technical facility integrated to near perfection. This
orchestra is, of course, musical to the bone's marrow.[17]

This is not the place to conduct a survey of Karajan's Berlin
recordings but it must be said that the 1962 Beethoven cycle was a
tour de force, the finest of its kind since the Toscanini to which it
paid partial homage. But if the public expected from the Berliners
memorable Beethoven and even more memorable Brahms (a
Brahms cycle appeared in 1964), they were perhaps less prepared
for the miraculously fluid Debussy record that appeared in 1964—
La Mer and *Prélude à l'après-midi d'un faune* coupled with the
Second Suite from Ravel's *Daphnis et Chloé*—or recordings of
Sibelius's Fourth and Fifth symphonies that quite eclipsed the
earlier Philharmonia recordings, and the Shostakovich Tenth. After

17   Neville Cardus, 'Olympic Heights', *The Guardian*, 17 Apr. 1961.

the completion of the *Ring* cycle, the Berlin orchestra now able to compete in territory that was once the special preserve of its Viennese cousin, Karajan both consolidated and extended the repertory during the 1970s, the music-making continuing to intensify both tonally, and emotionally as Karajan became older and more and more subject to personal trials and privations. There were obvious, almost predictable, highlights: the works of Bruckner and Richard Strauss in their entirety, fine Schumann and Brahms cycles, the Honegger Second and Third symphonies, and some stylish, full-bodied late Mozart. But other things took people unawares: the set devoted to the music of the Second Viennese School, the Mahler Sixth, and in the fullness of time the great recordings of the Mahler Ninth and a fine Nielsen Fourth. And there were some further unexpected and perhaps even now neglected delights: the early Tchaikovsky symphonies, a winningly alfresco Schubert cycle with an account of the 'Unfinished' as deep, dark, and grim as a late canvas by Tintoretto, and Haydn's Paris and London symphonies played with a proper Haydnish robustness and wit.

Yet Karajan soon exhausts even the chronicler's staying power. To list the symphonic achievements with the Berlin Philharmonic is to risk neglecting the opera recordings and, beyond them, Karajan's work in the theatre itself. In September 1965, Walter Legge told readers of *Musical America*: 'The American public will have no idea of Karajan's full stature as a conductor until it has heard how this Klingsor of operatic conductors conjurs up his magic gardens.' Much of Karajan's operatic repertory has been recorded. There have been one or two irksome omissions—*Elektra*, *Die Frau ohne Schatten*, productions that were highlights of the Strauss centenary celebrations in Salzburg and Vienna in 1964—as well as one or two works that Karajan has recorded but not conducted in the theatre since Ulm or Aachen. But, as Legge suggested, recordings are in this instance no substitute for the real thing. Karajan was by instinct and training a man of the theatre and it is another of those paradoxes surrounding his career that this central aspect of his art has to some extent been obscured from the general public gaze. True, the famous *Lucia di Lammermoor* with Callas visited Berlin, and the Salzburg *Ring* found its way briefly to New York; but

Karajan's work in the opera-house since 1950 was largely confined to Salzburg, Vienna, and, for a number of years, Milan. There are practical reasons why this has been so, but the effect was to make Salzburg, Easter or Summer, something of a place of pilgrimage. To hear Karajan in the opera-house the mountain has had to go to Mahomet.

Most people who made the pilgrimage found it well worth their while, not only for the quality of the music-making but also for a quality of staging and design that pointedly bypassed the often musically ruinous fads of post-war directors' opera in order to re-establish contact with an older and still valid tradition that goes back, with a passing glance at the work of Wieland Wagner, through Gründgens and Reinhardt to Roller and Mahler and, in some respects, Wagner himself. Since the early 1940s, Karajan frequently both conducted and directed.[18] Again, this was no act of vanity or calculated lust for power. Rather, it re-enacts the ideal of the Wagnerian *Gesamtkunstwerk*. As Peter Conrad has put it, 'Karajan doubles as director so that he can reproduce musical motifs on-stage.'[19] One of Karajan's simplest musico-dramatic experiments was his staging of the Callas *Lucia* in Milan in 1954. Franco Zeffirelli, one of the few directors with whom Karajan collaborated, recalled: 'Karajan didn't even try to direct. He just arranged everything around her. She did the Mad Scene with a follow-spot like a ballerina against black. Nothing else. He let her be music, absolute music.'[20]

It was Karajan's concern with 'music, absolute music'—'drama-made-music' rather than 'music-drama', to use Professor Kivy's useful distinction—that linked his work in the opera-house with his work in the concert-hall and, indeed, with his whole philosophical position. The yearning for wholeness, for oneness, is consistent with some of the tenets of both Buddhism and nineteenth-century German Romantic philosophy, to which Karajan was evidently drawn both by background and by temperamental inclination.

As early as 1938, Irmgard Seefried, then a young soprano in

---

18   See below, pp. 151–3.
19   Peter Conrad, *A Song of Love and Death: The Meaning of Opera* (London, 1987), 310.
20   Quoted in John Ardoin and Gerald Fitzgerald, *Callas* (London, 1974), 24.

Aachen, noted Karajan's inclination to use voices instrumentally, not wilfully or undramatically, but as part of a deeper process of aligning the musical and dramatic elements within the score. Unfortunately, since theatre direction is in many ways an ephemeral art, we can never really know how the famous Gründgens/Karajan *Zauberflöte* really looked and sounded in Berlin in 1938, though the production was celebrated at the time for the uncanny matching of musical and visual textures. And since Karajan's 1977 production of Strauss's *Salome* was not filmed we cannot recapture that with any certainty, though it exists in purely aural form on record.

Of course, not all operas are ideally suited to such treatment, but Karajan's stage productions tended to centre on repertoire that is itself within this tradition of the *Gesamtkunstwerk*: above all, the works of Wagner, Richard Strauss, Debussy, certain Puccini operas, and, perhaps more controversially, Verdi. Much of the music is night-orientated (quips about the darkness of Karajan's stagings miss this obvious point) and death-haunted. Indeed, for this reason one can usefully add Mozart's *Don Giovanni* and Bizet's *Carmen* to the above list: the use (in land-locked, mountainous Salzburg) of a nocturnal seascape as the backdrop to Act III of *Carmen* was one of Karajan's strangest and yet most haunting intimations of eternity. In 1962, Karajan staged and conducted Debussy's *Pelléas et Mélisande* in Vienna. According to H. C. Robbins Landon, it was the *Tristan und Isolde* shortly before that, a production of swarming darkness and rare musical sensibility, that had been for many people one of the greatest of all their musical experiences. But the Debussy, wonderfully evoked in a lengthy review by Cardus, demonstrates equally well what can be achieved when music, design, and stage movement are perfectly congruent. To quote one representative paragraph:

I can make no better compliment to Karajan, the Vienna State Opera Orchestra, and the singers than to say that all these instrinsic qualities of the work, not generally understood, were brought home. I confess that more than once I came near to tears, eyes as misted as the beautiful stage settings of Günther Schneider-Siemssen. The opening forest scene was an endless world of high trees, alluring and mysterious. The fountain in the park was an enchantment, with the orchestra at the beginning iridescent, all seen in reflection from afar. What magic of tone-chemistry is here! Different but in perfect harmony was the grotto scene, dark and the darkness more and more revealed when a glow of the outer night entered. The settings mingled with Maeterlinck and Debussy invisibly; the whispering wind, echoes and shadows, all the invisible shaping powers in a love tragedy that comes to a cruel climax because of the chattering of an innocent child . . .[21]

Günther Schneider-Siemssen was Roller to Karajan's Mahler for over a quarter of a century. Happily, his work is lavishly chronicled in illustrated books. The 1976 Salzburg Easter Festival *Lohengrin*, the designs based on fourteenth-century illuminated manuscripts and lit with a rare luminous aura, must rank as one of the most beautiful of all Wagner productions in recent memory; but, in a sense, it is invidious to single out this rather than the *Ring* or the *Tristan*, the *Parsifal*, or even the menacingly spectacular designs, half real, half fantastic, for the 1982 production of *Der fliegende Holländer*.

Singers' veneration of Karajan is well known; many, like the tenor José Carreras, have said that he has transformed their understanding of the art they serve. If there has been a criticism, it is that he often lured artists into singing roles beyond their immediate range or capacity. Sometimes he had to take 'no' for an answer; Jon Vickers declined to sing Tristan at the age of 30, though he would later sing Tristan for Karajan in Salzburg in 1972. But those who knew Karajan best have rarely questioned his judgement or good will in casting for his own productions. The problem has arisen when the singer has been tempted to take the performance to other places where the context has been less helpful: rushed schedules, routine conducting. The fact is, Karajan was able to accommodate and support voices, even in the most taxing roles, in a way that other conductors with a less complete control of the orchestra find it hard to emulate.

The Easter Festival has added a new dimension to Salzburg's musical life; though there are those who argue that Karajan changed the Summer Festival: both its audience and its artistic

<hr/>

21   Neville Cardus, 'A Compliment to Debussy', *The Guardian*, 15 Jan. 1962, reprinted in *Cardus on Music*, ed. Donald Wright (London, 1988), 309–11.

ideals. In fact, as Stephen Gallup has pointed out in a recent history of the festival, Karajan was the last surviving link with the traditions of the festival's founding fathers. During the Karajan years Mozart and Richard Strauss were not squeezed out, though the music of other composers was brought in. In his own particular way, Karajan also kept intact the ideal of ensemble opera, building teams and rehearsing, with the aid of handsome subventions from his record companies who make preliminary recordings, over a time-span that makes even Glyndebourne's schedules look rushed. It is expensive, of course. But it is difficult to find a major summer festival that is not expensive and, for want of seats, exclusive to those with the will, the guile, or the contacts with which to acquire tickets. In this, Salzburg is no different from Bayreuth or Glyndebourne or the fledgeling Rossini Festival in Pesaro, where first-night tickets comfortably outstrip Salzburg's. If there was a drawback to this grand strategy, it is that some of the gramophone recordings in recent years have lacked the startling intensity and insights of the theatre performances they have helped to prepare.

In the end, it is the technology of radio, the gramophone, television, and film that allows most of the barriers to be transcended, which is why Karajan, an élitist with a yearning to reach the widest possible international audience, invested so much of his time and his money in the quest for the high-quality dissemination of music to a world-wide audience. And yet in this area, too, Karajan has been subject to rebarbative questioning and criticism, not least on the grounds that an interest in technology is somehow incompatible with a man's credibility as a performing musician. In the early 1960s an American writer dubbed Karajan the conductor of 'mathematicians [Bach would probably have been flattered by such an appellation] and engineers'. And, on a slightly wider front, Chesterman, in his CBC interview, admitted to finding 'bothersome' Karajan's inexhaustible interest in the whys and wherefores of science, technology, and the ultimate questions of life and death. (In his reply, Karajan pointed out that as two men had died whilst conducting *Tristan und Isolde*, both more or less in the same place in the score, it was perhaps worth sponsoring some medical research into the subject.) The attitude of many older

musicians and critics to science and technology is nothing more, of
course, than the stale residue of the romantic, *fin de siècle* aesthetic
that, in the phrase of Villiers de L'Isle-Adam, claims science to be
'the religion of the suburbs'. In fact, Karajan's father was a doctor.
On his father's side of the family was a line of distinguished
academics mainly in philological disciplines. Karajan himself, not
unnaturally for the son of a doctor being educated in the second
and third decades of the twentieth century, had a training that
mixed science with the humanities. For the sake of prudence in an
age afflicted by mass unemployment, his parents urged him to
study practically, and for a year in Vienna Karajan studied
engineering, before decamping to his real vocation, music.

Historically, Karajan is a conductor of pivotal significance,
steeped as a child and as a young man in music-making of the great
Austro-German tradition, but the first great conductor to be reared
in the twentieth century's brave new technological age. (He is
pivotal in other ways too, not least culturally, with Austrian roots
and Slav and Mediterranean forebears.) It is tempting perhaps to
think musicians were innocent of technology at least until the age
of the LP and stereophonic sound. Yet in 1928, whilst Karajan was
studying at the Musikhochschule in Vienna, Schoenberg was telling
Erwin Stein:

In radio broadcasting a small number of sonic entities suffice for the
expression of all artistic thoughts; the gramophone and the various
mechanical instruments are evolving such clear sonorities that one will be
able to write much less heavily instrumented pieces for them.

That same year, Schoenberg completed his Variations for
Orchestra, Op. 31, which Karajan would one day remove from the
concert-hall to the recording studio to make one of the artistically
most successful and technologically most radical of all twentieth-
century gramophone recordings.

But old assumptions run deep and die hard. Sixty years after
Schoenberg was making those remarks and nearly twenty years
since Karajan made his recording of the Op. 31 Variations, it is still
possible to meet the argument that the gramophone can never be a
substitute for the sound of 'the real thing' in the concert-hall.
When Chesterman put to Karajan the proposition that concert-hall

sound was naturally superior to recorded sound, Karajan replied, 'For whom?' For a privileged few, perhaps, with access to an appropriate hall and the good fortune to find the right seat for the particular kind of music on offer. The lure of live music-making is, of course, irresistible: the sense of occasion, of which Karajan was himself a great provider, the throng of music-madded fans and *aficionados*, not to mention that bear-baiting element Glenn Gould was always so amusing about, as soloists are led out and put to their instruments before the attentive crowd. These elaborate rituals are nowhere more evident than in London's Henry Wood Promenade Concerts, perhaps the world's greatest music festival. And yet if you want properly to *hear* a Prom there is often little alternative but to stay at home with the radio transmission, so wretched are the acoustics in large areas of the Royal Albert Hall.

Unlike Glenn Gould—in many matters one of Karajan's great soul-mates—Karajan did not abandon the concert-giving habit; but, like Gould, he did unashamedly embrace recording technology to the full, the first conductor to do so in the wake of Stokowski, that would-be musico-technological pioneer who had the misfortune to be born thirty years too soon. In the post-war years, Karajan worked extensively with two of the world's most enterprising record producers, Walter Legge and John Culshaw. Culshaw reckoned that Karajan, and Benjamin Britten, were his two most intelligent studio artists. Certainly, the multi-studio techniques used for the famous 1959 Decca *Aida* were meat and drink to Karajan; and although he sometimes thought he knew more than he did, occasionally putting paid to expensive equipment, his mastery was of an order not previously seen in a working musician.

In the studio, in the early days of tape and LP, Karajan and Legge took immense care, not only over microphone placing and instrumental balance (some of their old mono recordings sound positively stereophonic), but also over the general artistic ambience. The perennial fascination of Karajan's 1954 recordings of Mozart's *Così fan tutte* and Strauss's *Ariadne auf Naxos* lies partly in the exquisitely cast singing and playing, partly in the use Legge and Karajan made of studio conditions to create performances of radical intimacy, the music-making addressed to the microphone and the private listener rather than belted out across some putative theatrical footlights.

Legge was, of course, a pragmatist. When Flagstad could not manage a high C in the 1952 Furtwängler recording of Wagner's *Tristan und Isolde*, Elisabeth Schwarzkopf sang it instead. And Karajan, in this as in many other things, was of a similar mind to Legge. For many people at the time such practices were regarded as immoral. Gould always argued that this perception of the use of recording technology divided by generation. In an amiable parody of an interview he once heard being given by Sir Adrian Boult, Gould spelt out the attitude to recording of that older generation: roughly, 'I don't mind doing the occasional recording, old boy— not everyone gets to concerts—and we'll do our best, but I don't want any "patching", we must keep the long line intact'. As a master of the long line himself, Karajan would probably have endorsed some of Boult's sentiments (many of Karajan's recordings have been put down more or less in a series of single takes), but he would also have agreed to an extent with Gould that 'good splices' can also 'build good lines'.[22] Gould, in fact, saw the objections to tape-editing as being rooted much more deeply in the assumption that man is his own best advocate—the most unwarranted assumption of the post-Renaissance era, Gould adds—with a consequent belief that such technological sleight of hand was, if not immoral, then certainly dehumanizing.

And moral outrage at the use of simple expedients can still run high. Not the least surprising aspect of the BBC radio documentary 'The Price of Perfection' was the space it gave to the aggrieved reminiscences of the Philharmonia Orchestra's former first flute, Gareth Morris. In November 1952 Karajan made what was at the time a celebrated recording of Bach's B minor Mass. In its grace, fire, and expressive fluency it was in some ways an important transition between the old Teutonic Bach style of the nineteenth century and what we expect now from the so-called authenticity movement. Alec Robertson, writing in *Gramophone*, hailed the recording as 'a landmark in the history of the gramophone'. Not

22   Glenn Gould, 'Music and Technology', *Piano Quarterly*, Winter 1974–5, reprinted in *The Glenn Gould Reader*, ed. Tim Page (London, 1987), 356.

least among the set's glories was the obbligato wind playing,
including a ravishing, long-breathed account of the flute solos in
the 'Domine Deus' by Morris himself. To help create a long line
and obviate intrusive snatched breaths, Karajan hired an additional
flautist to cover at least one of the notorious joins in the line.
Morris, it seems, has never forgiven Karajan for this piece of
seeming musical dissimulation which he evidently regarded, and
still regards, as a moral outrage. Naturally, such a tale of musical
turpitude sat well at the centre of a rather glibly (and often
inaccurately) assembled documentary devoted to the somewhat
tendentious premiss of its headline-catching title; but it illustrates,
too, how muddled and superficial—not to say unpleasingly
moralistic—thinking on these matters can be.

It used to be said—in the face of evidence of a growing and
changing repertory of enormous size—that Karajan was interested
in technology because after so many years in the business he had
exhausted his interest in the music itself. Culshaw, who knew
Karajan better than any of these armchair pundits, noted that since
Karajan had never been interested in interpretation for
interpretation's sake—which perhaps helps explain why his readings
often outlast those of more 'personalized' rivals—he naturally
diverted his attention to new projects, musical, technological,
scientific, logistical, until circumstances or new thinking drew him
back to the central repertoire that he had recorded earlier, with
other orchestras, other technology. In fact, by the mid-1970s,
Karajan's reputation and authority were such that he was to
become a central player in effecting the greatest of all musico-
technological revolutions of our times, the switch from LP to the
laser-tracking compact disc.

Compact disc technology had been available for some time, but
the quadraphonic experiment had failed and videotape technology
was in something of an impasse. Sony's President, Karajan's great
friend Akio Morita, was aware that the compact disc could not be
launched until the moment was ripe. In this Karajan proved the
catalyst everyone had been waiting for. Whilst the record
companies sat on their hands, nervous of another quadraphonic-
style fiasco, Karajan announced after seeing the new technology as
a working prototype that he would make no new recordings and

sign no new contracts with any company that was not committed
to digital recording and the earliest possible launch of the compact
disc. Whilst one of Karajan's recording companies held back, the
Deutsche Grammophon–Polygram group took the plunge. At the
1981 Salzburg Easter Festival, the Herbert von Karajan Foundation
in Salzburg teamed up with Sony, Philips, and the Polygram group
to announce the imminent launch of the compact disc. The rest is
history.

Even before the compact disc was finally launched to the general
public, however, Karajan was making yet another move. More or
less since the end of the Second World War, Karajan had been
fascinated by the challenge of music on film. Now, forty years on,
there was at last the technology—laser-tracking CD video—that
would give him the finest sound with the finest picture-resolution
in a medium that was compatible with the new domestic sound
system that would, by the early 1990s, render the LP largely
obsolete. Making and editing getting on for fifty films would take
time, but Karajan was well ahead of the game. His only problem
was, would he survive long enough to see through what was in
some ways the most monumental task he had yet set himself? It
was to prove a wretchedly difficult period. In 1982 the Berlin
Philharmonic rebelled over the attempt to appoint the clarinettist
Sabine Meyer. There was a recurrence of earlier back trouble and
more operations. Later, the press was able to seize avidly on some
tactlessly conceived marketing strategies for the eventual release of
the films. But Karajan's will was superhuman where music is
concerned and he always had in his hand a trump card: a capacity
for inner detachment that left him free of bitterness or rancour for
all that has been written and said about him over the years. I had
not seen him since 1982, but when we met again in his home near
Salzburg in March 1988 to record radio and television interviews on
the occasion of his 80th birthday he was quite unchanged, as
courteous and welcoming as ever and perfectly settled within
himself. Karajan was not a saint, but he had the patience and inner
calm of one. And by 1988 his mission was largely accomplished.

He learnt the film-making craft, finally, in the 1960s with the
French director Henri-Georges Clouzot. Again, as early as 1969, it
was Glenn Gould who, having seen some of the early Karajan/

Clouzot films of orchestral and choral music, rejoiced at their imaginative refutation of what he called the 'proscenium psychology'.[23] By scorning concert-hall constants, Karajan was making a realistic attempt to put music on film. It will be clear, I think, to anyone reading what Karajan has to say in Chapter 6 of these *Conversations* that his is an enterprise of particular historical significance. For the first time, a major interpretative musician has equipped himself with the necessary skills to mastermind his own visualization of the music he conducts, which allows him, in the process, to offer a new generation of music-lovers a sophisticated set of options for the study and appreciation of music in performance.

It is a typical Karajan project because in one respect it is enormously sophisticated—the technology is elaborate, expensive, and bang up to date—and in another it is very simple, inasmuch as its ultimate aim is nothing more or less than the lucid presentation of the music. Of course, it is a record of Karajan's own latter-day conducting technique, and to some extent his own personal monument; it is also a record of the work of one of the greatest orchestras ever assembled. But watching the films being edited down, I found myself studying neither Karajan nor the orchestra. I found myself, by a curious alchemy of eye and ear, wondering at things in *Don Quixote* and Brahms's Second Symphony that I had neither noticed nor pondered before. The films are fascinating documents; but they are more besides. Since Karajan was first and foremost a great musician, it follows that Karajan the film-maker is a man who helps transform our aural sensibilities.

23   Glenn Gould, ' "Oh, for heaven's sake, Cynthia, there must be something else on!" ', *Musical America*, Apr. 1969, reprinted in *Glenn Gould Reader*, ed. Page, 372–3. Though Karajan broke the 'proscenium psychology' with these films of the late 1960s, he later rejected the high level of conductor-orientation in them as well as the formalized and depersonalized filming of the orchestra. The decision of several European TV stations to show his old Unitel film of Beethoven's *Eroica* Symphony as a memorial tribute would not have amused him.

Conversations with
Von Karajan

1 · The Formative Years

RO Your first public conducting engagement was in Salzburg on 23 January 1929. You had organized it yourself shortly after graduating from the conducting class at the Musikhochschule in Vienna?

HvK Yes, with the help of one or two friends. My father played the clarinet in the orchestra; he was a good amateur musician. His particular specialism was the bass clarinet. Up to that time I had very limited opportunities to conduct and I very much wanted to direct a real concert. I knew the Mozarteum Orchestra because I had played with them as a pianist, and I was well known in Salzburg, so we had no difficulty in selling tickets. People were curious to see what I could do.

RO What was the programme?

HvK Strauss's *Don Juan*, followed by a Mozart piano concerto with a young girl called Pessl as soloist—she later went to the United States—and Tchaikovsky's Fifth Symphony.

RO And was the concert generally well received?[1]

HvK I think so. I was offered work at the opera-house in Ulm immediately afterwards.

RO Walter Legge[2] liked to tell the story—I think as an example of both your musicianship and your tactical skills—that at the graduation class in Vienna you chose the Overture to Rossini's *Guillaume Tell* and then sent everyone away except the cellos so you could show exactly what you could do with them in the opening bars of the piece.

HvK That's not quite true. We did have a short time to show off

1 A review in the local Salzburg paper was favourable and suggests a good deal of the Karajan we were later to know. The conducting was said to be refined and impassioned, with a natural feel for musical architecture, and an avoidance of anything vulgar or emptily theatrical. Even at the age of 19, Karajan was said to rely not on histrionics, but on persuasion and the suggestive power of gesture.

2 Walter Legge (1906–79) was Karajan's principal recording producer in Vienna and later in London from 1946 to 1960. The Philharmonia Orchestra, founded by Legge, was Karajan's principal concert and recording orchestra in the early 1950s.

Karajan's birthplace by the Makartsteg in
Salzburg

whatever skills we had managed to acquire. Most students liked to talk a lot because they thought it would impress the professors. In fact, I decided to concentrate on the end of the Overture, the 'allegro vivace'. The orchestra was not playing it in time, so I made them rehearse it at a slower tempo. We were examined by the Director of the Musikhochschule, Franz Schmidt;[3] he had recently taken over.

RO   You had been playing the piano in public in Salzburg since 1918, when you were barely ten years old, and you went on to play Mozart piano concertos and Liszt Hungarian Rhapsodies in public concerts. And there had also been for many years the musical evenings at your parents' home.

HvK   My brother and I were able to attend these from a very early age, and take part in them,[4] though they would sometimes go on until the early hours of the morning. My father was a doctor in the local hospital, so he would sometimes be called away during the evening. But there was never any question of us finishing when he went or while he was away. Everyone had to wait until he returned. I met a lot of people at my parents' house, including many people of real ability, and that I was always grateful for.

RO   Your father was evidently very serious about music-making and your musical studies. Was it a very strict regime at home?

HvK   My father was not pleased when he came back early or unexpectedly from the hospital and found that we were out drinking or talking to girls. Drink, girls, these things were very much disapproved of. My mother was very kind—she was very fond of music, of Wagner in particular—but I don't think our

3   Franz Schmidt (1874–1939), composer, conductor, Director of the Vienna Musikhochschule from 1927 to 1931. His music, including four symphonies, is increasingly highly regarded. The Intermezzo from his opera *Notre Dame* brought him international fame; Karajan has recorded it three times.

4   Notes kept by Karajan's father show the 9-year-old Herbert joining in an eight-hand piano performance of Haydn's Symphony No. 103, 'Drum roll', on Sunday, 15 April 1917, and four days later a performance of Mendelssohn's Symphony No. 3, with Dr von Karajan noting with approval the technical accuracy and good rhythm of his younger son's playing.

parents found it very easy to understand my brother and myself, especially as we had our own private language which no one could work out.

RO   There was school, and a lot of sport, and time spent in the mountains; but music was clearly something of a priority.

HvK   I would practise the piano for three or four hours a day. In the end I was unable to go any further with it because of an inflamed tendon in one of my hands.

RO   I suspect that even in those days you were a workaholic.

HvK   I wanted to make a career for myself outside Salzburg. Yes, even then it was a question of work, work, work, and more work.

RO   As a student in Vienna you were obviously highly motivated, but as far as conducting went there wasn't much direct instruction?

HvK   My piano teacher, Professor Hofmann—not the famous pianist, another man—had suggested I consider conducting seriously. Clemens Krauss had taught classes in the past but he had left the whole thing in the hands of a Professor Wunderer and a man from the Vienna Philharmonic who was interested in conducting but hadn't the slightest idea how to go about it. So we were on our own. We formed a group among ourselves and used to meet and play through the works that were being performed at the Opera that next day—two pianos, four pianists, some singers, a small chorus. We improvised our own performances and took turns at conducting as well.

RO   You obviously made quite an impression personally at the time. In Gregor von Rezzori's story *Troth* the music-loving and very courageous Jewish girl Minka Raubitschek often has a gifted young man called Herbert von Karajan to play the piano at her parties. Did you know Gregor von Rezzori?

HvK   Yes, I remember him very well, but much later. In Munich, I think.[5]

5   *Troth* originally appeared in the *New Yorker* in September 1967 and later formed part of Rezzori's *Memoirs of an Anti-Semite* (London, 1981).

Top, left: Karajan's father

Top, right: Karajan's mother

Bottom: Karajan with his brother Wolfgang and friends in front of his house in Salzburg, 1919

RO The tuition in the conducting class may have been poor but Vienna had a very rich concert and operatic life at the time. Were you able to get to hear all the Richard Strauss and Clemens Krauss and Furtwängler concerts?

HvK I heard everything at the Opera and Musikverein. My uncle was in charge of various technical and security matters at the Opera, so he always had two tickets for every event. There was also a great deal of experimental music. When Webern conducted student concerts I often found myself caught up in the riots.

RO As far as the Opera was concerned, Mahler had long gone; but did you see any of Roller's work?[6]

HvK Not his early work, of course, but many of his productions in Salzburg in the 1920s. They were magnificent; in particular I remember a *Don Giovanni* with Duhan as the Don.[7]

RO Various conductors were in charge of that particular production; first Richard Strauss, and later Muck and Schalk. How much did you see of Schalk at that time?[8]

HvK I learnt a good deal from him. On the surface he was a very matter-of-fact man, and he didn't at all like rehearsing; but he was a good musician. I don't think he was at all well known abroad but in Austria he was famous for his wit. I remember at one rehearsal the Don Giovanni came on stage in a rather bizarre costume. Schalk was at the piano. He didn't say a word; instead, he played very quietly a short quotation from an opera which said all that needed to be said. To some extent, I think his wit was a mask. People who didn't like him said he was very sarcastic, but he

6 Alfred Roller (1864–1935), Austrian painter and stage-designer, famous for his collaborations with Mahler and Richard Strauss.

7 A Vienna State Opera production first seen in Salzburg on 14 August 1922, conducted by Richard Strauss. Franz Schalk conducted the 1927 Salzburg revival, again with Duhan as Don Giovanni.

8 Franz Schalk (1863–1931), Austrian conductor, pupil of Bruckner. Conducted in London and New York 1898–1911 but was otherwise heard mostly in Vienna, where he conducted the première of Strauss's *Die Frau ohne Schatten*, 1919, and Salzburg.

always seemed to me to be a most sensitive and competent man.[9]

RO   Max Reinhardt[10] was the presiding genius, theatrically speaking. Did you work with him?

HvK   I was able to watch his work all the time. I was a kind of maid of all works: conducting, coaching, taking chorus rehearsals. He understood that you can never change a singer's personality to fit a role. If you try, you will end up with an imitation of yourself.

RO   Were there other theatre producers you admired at the time?

HvK   Felsenstein, though that was later, in Aachen.[11] I mention him in particular because he understood that opera concerns those ecstatic moments when a man or a woman has to use a means of expression other than the spoken word. Many directors who come to opera from the theatre are incapable of understanding this quite special form of human expression.

RO   But the Aachen *Falstaff* was your only collaboration.

HvK   The first and the last! What I found less acceptable was his desire to chisel every character into the precise image he had conceived of

9   Bruno Walter (1876–1962) has written of Schalk in much the same terms as Karajan speaks of him here: 'He was a Viennese, filled with the local musical tradition, a man of spirit and culture—and he loved the Vienna Opera . . . His achievements as director of the institute deserve to be held in the highest esteem. He was a man of fighting disposition, the possessor of an exceedingly nimble and mischievous wit, and he used his sharp weapons effectively in the interest of the State Opera and art' (*Theme and Variations* (London, 1947), 302–3).

10   Max Reinhardt (1873–1943), Austrian theatre producer and founder in 1920, with Richard Strauss and Hugo von Hofmannsthal, of the Salzburg Festival, where he oversaw the morality play *Jedermann* and major theatre productions of plays by Shakespeare, Goldoni, Schiller, and Goethe until he was driven into exile after the 1937 festival. For the 1933 production of Part I of Goethe's *Faust*, Karajan directed the music specially composed for the production by Bernhard Paumgartner.

11   Walter Felsenstein (1901–75), Austrian producer. His insistence that singing on stage must seem to be 'a credible, convincing, authentic, and indispensable means of human expression' made him a radical and revered force in opera after the Second World War. His work was a good deal curtailed by the Third Reich's Reichstheaterkammer, though he worked with Karajan on the historically important production of Verdi's *Falstaff* in Aachen in 1941.

Top: Clemens Holzmeister's stage setting in the
Felsenreitschule for the 1933 Salzburg Festival
production of Goethe's *Faust*

Bottom: Max Reinhardt (*left*) with Bernhard
Paumgartner at a rehearsal for the 1933 Salzburg
Festival production of Goethe's *Faust*

it. In the end, we were left with eleven versions of Felsenstein walking around the stage. In this he was the opposite of Reinhardt.

RO   With some notable exceptions, directors have been distrusted by you.

HvK   The problem is, when you have conducted a piece for many years you have a knowledge of the interior musical structures that are closed to most theatre directors.

RO   Was Gründgens[12] an exception to this general rule?

HvK   He was one of the most interesting men I worked with in my early years. He was a musician to his fingertips and he had a very subtle understanding of the interplay of characters on the stage. We had a very happy collaboration in Berlin over Mozart's *Die Zauberflöte*, which he had been wanting to do for a number of years.[13] Papageno's very sensual character was explored through his relationship to his antitypes, Pamina and Tamino.

RO   He had made his name with two earlier Mozart productions at the Kroll Opera in Berlin with Klemperer. Klemperer, one gathers, thought the production of *Così fan tutte* over-elaborate. He wanted virtually no stage action.

HvK   I would not stage it at all! Wonderful music, but in the theatre— well, I must say it is not to my taste.

RO   The production of *Le nozze di Figaro* which Gründgens did earlier

12   Gustaf Gründgens (1899–1963) was one of the outstanding German actors of his generation. A production of Cocteau's *Orphée* was seen by Klemperer, who invited Gründgens to direct Ravel's *L'Heure espagnole* in the 1929–30 season of Berlin's Kroll Opera. After the Second World War he was head of theatre companies in Düsseldorf and Hamburg. He produced Shakespeare's *As You Like It* (*Wie es Euch gefällt*) at the 1951 Salzburg Festival and was invited back to Salzburg in 1958 to direct a new production of Verdi's *Don Carlo* conducted by Karajan.

13   Berlin, 18 December 1938. The production was celebrated for its airy lightness and diaphanous mood and for the evident deference of the director to the sounds of Mozart's score. The matching of the stage pictures with the light, brilliant sound of the orchestra under the young Karajan was regarded as being something of a revolution in opera production of the period. Karajan's conducting was also praised for its 'authenticity'—e.g. the use of boys' voices in the Knabenterzett.

Gustaf Gründgens in rehearsal

with Klemperer in 1931 was said to be politically very radical, yet Gründgens later became Intendant of Berlin's Staatliches Schauspielhaus, with Goering's support.

HvK He took a very sceptical view of the Nazis. I remember during the rehearsals for *Die Zauberflöte* he criticized the Sarastro for putting on the kind of unctuous tone that, according to Gründgens, was best left to indoctrination meetings for the Party faithful.

RO You began, though, not in Berlin but in Ulm, in a tiny theatre.

HvK The stage was about six metres wide, the size of an average living-room.

RO And with a tiny orchestra. What was your first production?

HvK It was *Le nozze di Figaro*. But after the Salzburg concert I had been offered only a kind of 'trial', just one performance of someone else's production. I said, this is impossible. If I am to show what I can do I must be given a chance to make my own complete performance. Then someone fell out and it was possible for me to do the *Figaro* myself. And even with a small orchestra Mozart sounds well. Verdi also.

RO Neither the size of the orchestras nor the size of the stage seems to have deterred you from staging major works by Verdi—*Un ballo in maschera*, for instance, which you've now come back to after fifty years—Wagner, and Strauss. What kind of singers were you working with during these years?

HvK In a theatre like Ulm there was a shortage of good young basses and baritones but there were many fresh, unspoiled soprano voices. Many of the singers were what we call *verpflichtet*: they were contracted to do so many performances and they simply turned up and did them. When I did *Der Rosenkavalier*, the man down to sing Ochs came to me and said, 'I don't know this part.' So I said I would teach it to him. Then I discovered he couldn't read music.[14]

14 By no means uncommon then and later. When Giulini asked a world-famous mezzo-soprano in La Scala, Milan, in the 1950s to note the dots after the crotchets, she said, 'I don't read music: do you want it longer or shorter?'

So I taught it him at the piano—we had over one hundred sessions. So even now if you wake me at three o'clock in the morning and sing me one bar of *Der Rosenkavalier* I will be able to carry on from where you start! The great model for the role was Mayr;[15] every nuance and inflection of the role was marvellously explored by him and it was a constant source of fascination for us to study.

RO   He recorded extracts from the role, under Heger, I think.

HvK   Yes, but I remember Mayr with Clemens Krauss; this was a masterly realization of the score.

RO   The regime at Ulm was, in one respect, drudgery; in another, it was a phenomenal training.

HvK   We learnt everything from scratch. Nothing from gramophone records. Only the score and what we could work out on the piano and what we were able to hear in the opera-house from singers like Mayr. And in those days you had to have fifteen years' training before anyone would really look at you.

RO   This is something we must come back to—the whole question of how young conductors are best trained and developed—but I would like to ask you about your years in Aachen. The general story is well known:[16] the director at Ulm saying you must go to better things, your dismissal, months of unemployment, and then the chance of the Aachen post despite the fact that at 27 years of age you were thought far too young for such an important post in German musical life. What, apart from employment, was the great excitement about the Aachen post?

HvK   I think mainly that I had the chance to work with a very good choral society. I have a great love of the choral music repertory and

15   Richard Mayr (1877–1935), Austrian bass-baritone.

16   Karajan 'hypnotized' the Aachen Intendant into giving him an audition in June 1934; he conducted the overtures to *Oberon* and *Die Meistersinger* and the opening of Mozart's *Haffner* Symphony. In the Autumn he conducted Beethoven's *Fidelio*. After a tactical job-application to Karlsruhe, he displaced the scholar and conductor Peter Raabe as Aachen's General Music Director. Raabe, who was strongly pro-Nazi, was made President of the Reichsmusikkammer in 1935.

Karajan during his time in Ulm

my training would have been incomplete without it at this stage.

RO   Your interest in works like the B minor Mass of Bach, Beethoven's *Missa Solemnis*, and such semi-sacred works as the Bruckner Fifth Symphony was said not to have endeared you to certain Party officials.

HvK   They did not offer me works of comparable greatness as alternatives, so their objections were hardly a problem. The real problem was how to train the choir to sing these difficult works. Again, I remember a great many rehearsals, sixty or seventy each for the first performances of the Bach or the Beethoven. I have watched famous conductors direct this music and I know just from looking at their backs that in some passages they are no longer in control, they are terrified.

RO   Were there any choral conductors you especially admired?

HvK   There was a man called Jarov who fascinated me.[17] He had left Russia soon after the Revolution and brought with him a choir of *émigré* singers; they called themselves the Don-Kosaken-Chor. Jarov had a special technique. He grouped the singers very close to each other. He would give them the note; and then he would have a method of beating the rhythm for several bars and—and this was always remarkable—the choir would enter with a sound that had an unbelievable power and precision in the attack. I always attended their concerts to try and work out how he got this effect.

RO   It was in Ulm and perhaps in Aachen too that you developed your life-long aversion to small theatres?

HvK   Ever since then I have felt a terrible claustrophobia in a small theatre.

17   Sergei Jarov or Jaroff (1896–1985), Russian choral conductor. Trained at the Academy for Church Singing at the Imperial Synod. Served as a Cossack officer. Left Russia after the defeat of the White Russians in the immediate post-Revolutionary period. Formed the Don Cossack Choir. Recorded extensively in the 1930s and in the post-war period for Polydor, Brunswick, Deutsche Grammophon. Karajan incorporated the Choir into his famous 1966 Berlin recording of Tchaikovsky's *1812* Overture.

RO And a claustrophobia about bureaucrats, theatre managements, politicians, the Mr Tietjens and the Mr Hilberts. . . .?[18]

HvK Only one thing exhausts me and that is the red tape of bureaucrats. That is why I created my own festival in Salzburg each Easter. I am afraid I was not born to obey!

RO You helped to design[19] the Salzburg theatre. It is your ideal?

HvK In Salzburg we have the equipment; but more important, we have the people. This has become a place where the man who cares passionately for his craft—lighting or stage work—comes to show what he really can do. I once asked my stage director what would happen if I made an unexpected ritardando. He replied, 'Herr Karajan, do you imagine that I am not listening to what you are doing? If you make a ritardando, I retard my machine. It is very easy!' A lot of nonsense was talked about the new Festspielhaus. But, first, you can see the whole stage—and even today houses are being built with seats that have a view of only half the stage!—and second, it is acoustically marvellous for the audience and the conductor; for opera and for concerts, especially choral concerts. Some houses, like La Scala, are very good for opera but terrible for orchestral music. With our stage and our workshops, which are better than any theatre in the world, we are able to achieve really striking stage pictures; and they have nothing to do with these modern productions that do everything contrary to the music.

RO I can't think of anywhere that the stage designs have been more consistently imaginative and beautifully realized than in Salzburg

18 Heinz Tietjen (1881–1967) ran the German State Theatres, including Bayreuth, from 1930 to 1945. After the war he worked in London, Hamburg, and Bayreuth. A competent conductor and producer, he was a consummate administrative wheeler-dealer. He is brilliantly evoked by Bruno Walter in *Theme and Variations*, pp. 297–300, in a passage that addresses the often-asked question 'Did Tietjen ever live?': 'He would indulge in cordial conversation—ah, Tietjen was actually living, one thought—when, just as suddenly, the attack would disappear behind a mask of blankness.' Egon Hilbert, a survivor of Dachau, was a prominent figure, in Salzburg and Vienna, in the Austrian post-war artistic renaissance. Karajan engaged him as general manager of the Vienna State Opera but the partnership proved unsuccessful.

19 Opened 1960. Designed by Clemens Holzmeister, the architect of the original Festspielhaus and the Felsenreitschule but overseen in all essential details by Karajan.

over the last twenty years. They are there to see in various books
that have been published;[20] I suppose it is sad that they haven't
been seen by a wider opera-going public.

HvK   You see, I had a dream many years ago that the opera-houses of
the world would make many more exchanges. We took the *Ring* to
the Metropolitan Opera in New York, which was a partial success.
But there were problems with the orchestra . . . and perhaps,
looking back to it now, I was not always very helpful to Mr Bing,[21]
but, in general, the idea of co-operation between houses was not
welcomed. So I said, well, I have my thing here in Salzburg; if they
want to see it they must make the effort to come here.

RO   One of the details of the New Festspielhaus in Salzburg that people
like to gossip about was the fact that the orchestra pit could be
raised or lowered by you at the touch of a button. People then
sometimes criticized the balances.

HvK   There is a lot of nonsense talked about this. In the first place, I
always threatened the orchestra that if they played too loudly I
would simply lower them by ten centimetres; and if they
continued, then by the end of the first act they would be in the
dungeon. But it is important that in rehearsals and in performance
the singers and the players can hear one another. A woodwind solo
may be as important to the musical drama as a vocal entry, but we
can have both. The real problem is with the strings, which can blot
out a singer with thick, heavy sound. But I can make seventy
strings sound pianissimo. When we did the *Ring* people said it was
'chamber music'; but I would deny that. It was the full Wagner
orchestra, with full sonority, but played with real subtlety and the
full range of dynamic levels.

RO   I remember it very well. What I can't now work out is how as a
university student in England I managed to get tickets for *Das
Rheingold* and *Die Walküre* at those first Easter Festivals.

---

20   Often expensively. But see Peter Csobádi (ed.), *Karajan oder die kontrollierte Ekstase*
(Vienna, 1988), 50–6, 105–12, for some representative colour plates.
21   Sir Rudolf Bing (b. 1902), General Manager New York Metropolitan Opera 1950–72.

HvK I must have been subsidizing you. I made £9 profit the first year!

RO When you first went to Vienna to conduct at the State Opera in, I think, 1937, you saw the worst side of opera-house routine?

HvK That was the *Tristan*. Bruno Walter was there and afterwards I was offered the post of first kapellmeister; but I had to say, frankly I am better off in Aachen. I had been offered three rehearsals plus some sessions with the singers. We lost one rehearsal because Rossini's *Barbiere* had been cancelled and *Lohengrin* was being put on in its place. Then the Philharmonic had some crisis and claimed they needed an extra rehearsal elsewhere. Finally, I was left with one rehearsal, and at that point Professor Rosé, who was the distinguished leader of the orchestra in those days, came to me and said, 'Look here, you have only one rehearsal. You can't do anything with one rehearsal. Why not cancel it? If you do, I can assure you we shall be in your debt and we shall play for you as though you were Mahler himself.' Or perhaps it was Toscanini. Incredible!

RO What about the singers?

HvK The principal soprano was very happy to attend to her correspondence. But this is one of the experiences that taught me very early in my career that I must do the opposite. In Milan, in London with Walter Legge, in Vienna, and now in Salzburg I coach the singers myself. Over the years I have been able to spend many hours with individual singers. And here there can be real development. But then they can go away and sing in places where no one works with them and very quickly their talent can become spoilt.

RO Did you hear any of the great non-Austro-German conductors of the time?

HvK I heard Talich[22] a great deal. And I can say he had one of the

22 Václav Talich (1883–1961), the outstanding Czech conductor of his generation. Conductor of the Czech Philharmonic Orchestra from 1919 to 1941. Many recordings, including the complete *Má vlast* which Karajan particularly admired in live concert performances.

strongest of all influences on me. He was a very powerful man. He had what seemed to me a great genius for—how can I put it?— drawing the orchestra together and controlling it as a single expressive instrument. I was fascinated to watch this, particularly as at that time this is something I could not do myself. I tried to imitate it but I couldn't do it. So he left a very deep impression on me; it was something I knew I had to work towards in the years ahead.

RO   He sounds like a man in the great tradition of Hans Richter.

HvK   But with better results in terms of orchestral playing, perhaps. I once was engaged to conduct a concert in Mannheim and the pianist who had been engaged was Frederic Lamond.[23] I had on the programme Brahms's Fourth Symphony and at the rehearsal Lamond said to me, 'You know, I knew Brahms; I heard him conduct this piece.' You can imagine the effect this had on me. I was terrified. Later on there was a reception. Lamond was talking to some people and then as he was leaving he came by me and said, 'But, you know, it wasn't all as beautiful as you might imagine!' Some things at that time were no doubt very good; but I suspect if we could hear some of them now we simply would not tolerate them.

RO   What about Mengelberg?[24] He was, like Stokowski, a legendary orchestral trainer with an early interest in the gramophone.

HvK   I invited him to come and conduct the orchestra in Aachen. I prepared the orchestra very carefully, particularly for his jokes and set speeches, which I told them they must be amused by. When he arrived he asked, 'How many people in the orchestra?' They told him it was 108. 'So, I will say everything 108 times because no one

23 Frederic Lamond (1868–1948), Scottish pianist and composer. Studied in Frankfurt and with Liszt and von Bülow. Début Berlin 1885. His *Memoirs* (Glasgow, 1949) give vivid fragmented impressions of musicians he met and knew, including Brahms.

24 Willem Mengelberg (1871–1951) was conductor of the Amsterdam Concertgebouw Orchestra from 1895 to 1944. He gave first performances of important works by Strauss (*Ein Heldenleben* is dedicated to Mengelberg and his orchestra) and Mahler. One of the finest orchestral trainers of all time. His rehearsal methods are vividly evoked in Bernard Shore's *The Orchestra Speaks* (London, 1937), 111–25.

ever listens . . .'. The orchestra were able to laugh at this exactly on cue. He was a great disciplinarian. At the start of the rehearsal he saw one of the violinists playing in a slovenly way, with the neck of his instrument pointing towards the floor. 'And who are you playing to, my friend? Please make your music in the proper direction!'[25]

RO I know that, like a lot of ordinary concert-goers and record collectors, you are not very much impressed by the slimmed-down sound of the present generation of period-instrument performers; but your performances of the B minor Mass in the 1930s and '40s were regarded as being almost revolutionary, with very buoyant rhythms and slimmed-down textures.

HvK It was necessary to get away from a beer-hall style of singing these works. This was something I was able to develop very much when I was appointed as director for life of the Vienna Singverein. The problem with the period-instrument performances I have heard in recent times is a technical one: they do not play in tune. But I hear interesting things. There can be problems with something like the 'Quoniam' of the B minor Mass with the horn part that always sounds problematic on the modern instrument. I heard a performance conducted by Schreier which I liked very much. And there is the performance by Rifkin with just eight solo voices. Perhaps there is a middle way. The piece must not be too heavy but it must have a certain weight to it. I am planning performances with two sopranos and two basses sharing the soprano and bass arias so that the voices are really suited to the different vocal ranges. I have also been listening to this wonderful young singer from Dresden, Olaf Bär. I asked him how good his *pianissimo* was. He said: 'I can sing so quietly that from two metres you will not hear me!'

RO You have always preferred young voices: Schwarzkopf and Gedda on the 1952 recording of the B minor Mass that you made partly in Vienna with the Singverein and partly in London with the soloists.

25 A point Karajan often made to young players in an orchestra who may be looking a little casual.

In Milan in June 1950 you had Schwarzkopf; also Kathleen Ferrier as one of your soloists.

HvK I remember. It would be impossible for anyone who was there to forget her singing, particularly of the Agnus Dei.[26]

RO There was also Jurinac, Seefried . . .

HvK Seefried[27] began her career with me in Aachen. She was one of the most gifted singers I ever worked with. We did many productions together, particularly of Mozart and Richard Strauss—the *Ariadne*, of course. She died recently and I wrote a long letter to her husband, Wolfgang Schneiderhan. I felt it as a great loss because even after her retirement she remained a wonderful source of advice and inspiration to young singers. She belonged to a generation who had fine voices and who were also dramatically credible. They looked well on stage. This for me has always been important. When the fashion changed after the war, it was difficult for some older singers, just as it was for some of the stars of silent films when the talkies came in. I remember taking *Der Rosenkavalier* to Milan with Schwarzkopf and others. When I arrived at the rehearsal the leader of the orchestra said, 'Mr von Karajan, I am sorry but we cannot begin; the singers are not here.' 'They are on the stage', I told him. 'Those are singers?' he said. 'I thought they were ballet dancers!'[28]

26 EMI is said to possess tapes of this. Acting on behalf of Karajan and Wieland Wagner, Walter Legge tried to persuade Ferrier to sing the part of Brangäne in the 1952 Bayreuth Festival production of *Tristan und Isolde*. It is doubtful whether she would have accepted even if her health had permitted it.

27 Irmgard Seefried (1919–88), German soprano who worked in Aachen from 1939 to 1943 and then in Vienna, where she took the role of the Composer in the production of *Ariadne auf Naxos* staged, and recorded live, on 11 June 1944 in honour of Strauss's 80th birthday in the presence of the composer. Her 1954 studio recording, conducted by Karajan, is now on CD.

28 As a young soprano living in Aachen, Elisabeth Grümmer was stunned to be engaged by Karajan for Lortzing's *Der Wildschütz*, for Alice in Verdi's *Falstaff* (the Felsenstein production), and Oktavian in *Der Rosenkavalier*: 'Believe it or not, as I learned later, my being given Oktavian was entirely due to my legs, because Karajan always had a great sense of the character looking just right, and he felt that my legs, in knee breeches, would fit correctly into the picture' (Lanfranco Rasponi, *The Last Prima Donnas* (New York, 1975; London, 1984), 111).

RO   You had some access to the Berlin Philharmonic after 1939 for the occasional recording, despite Furtwängler's jealousy, also the Berlin Staatskapelle, and occasional opportunities to work with, say, the Amsterdam Concertgebouw Orchestra. Equally, to get work during the war you had to settle for less distinguished outfits, like the Turin Radio Symphony Orchestra. How by that stage in your career did you tolerate bad orchestras?

HvK   I can tell you quite frankly. I heard in my inner ear what I wanted to hear and the rest . . . well, it went down! But there can be moments when your inner ear is astonished by what comes out. With a big orchestra after a certain time, if they are used to you and really play as they can, they will sometimes give you something more beautiful than you thought you could hear. And then the *real* work begins, to work it up to a higher and higher level, and this surely cannot be done until you have fifteen or twenty years working with the one orchestra. This is the reason why I said to the managers of the Berlin Philharmonic in 1955, I will have the orchestra for my lifetime, otherwise I will not sign the contract. And this pays in the results you get only after a very long time.

RO   The regime of working with less than first-rate orchestras is beneficial, though, as part of a conductor's training?

HvK   Working with bad orchestras can be a wonderful lesson. If you can make a bad orchestra tolerable, that is valuable. And as orchestras, even good ones, always make mistakes in the same places, you carry over a lot of experience. Then there are some very talented conductors who cannot do anything with a really top orchestra. They are wonderful with good or very good orchestras, but with a top orchestra they seem to have both hands bound! It is a kind of malediction. So nowadays I am sometimes worried when a young conductor goes straight to the Vienna Philharmonic.[29] What I have

29   Karajan first conducted the Vienna Philharmonic—a programme of Debussy and Ravel—in 1934 at the age of 26; but he was 38 by the time he came to work regularly with them.

said to our young prize-winners[30] is, don't be complacent. You are good but soon I am going to throw into your back a whole phalanx of new ones. We all thrive on competition; without it nothing happens. In the meantime, a new generation of conductors is being born; which is good because some of us are getting quite old now!

RO   Your conductors' competitions brought on some new talent, beginning with the Finnish conductor Okko Kamu, who won the first competition in 1969; and you've been a great help to most of the new generation of top conductors—Abbado, Ozawa, and so on. But isn't there a danger that your help and endorsement can accelerate a career too quickly?

HvK   It is difficult to tell. In all these things you have to wait ten or fifteen years. People can come to expect too much of someone who suddenly has great success. They say they have never heard anything like it. It is a miracle. He conducts great concerts, and before long he will make the lame walk—and then he does just a good concert and people are disappointed.

RO   Would you have valued a little more help when you were starting?

HvK   I looked for it and never found it. You see, the people were so remote, like gods. I was 45 before I spoke with Toscanini and then he attacked me for doing Debussy's *Pelléas et Mélisande* at La Scala in French. 'You might as well do *Il trovatore* in German,' he said. We laughed. But, it is true, there was no help and in many places quite a lot of opposition. And because of this, I have always been determined to do the contrary. I know there is a theory that great qualities will always reveal themselves in the end. But you can spare *very* much trouble because there are times when you can say to someone, 'At this point, you are going in the wrong direction.'

RO   And you were presented as Furtwängler's rival.

HvK   People say we didn't get on but the fact is, we hardly ever met. I attended his rehearsals whenever I could. Legge brought us

30   Of the conducting competition Karajan launched in Berlin in the late 1960s.

Seiji Ozawa with Karajan. At the same
time as winning the Koussevitsky Prize
in Boston in 1960, Ozawa also won a
scholarship to study with Karajan in
Berlin

Top: Karajan with the Städtisches Orchester, Aachen

Bottom: Karajan conducting in Aachen in 1939

together after the war. Furtwängler was very sullen but musicians like to joke and tell stories and the evening was a great success. I had the impression, though, that he was not a happy man.

RO Your difficulties multiplied almost in inverse proportion to your developing experience during the early 1940s. Journalists and critics seem to be fixated on the war years. You managed to stay in work but, given the vast resources and prestige attached to music-making in the Third Reich, your career didn't exactly flourish. How long did you manage to stay in Aachen?

HvK As long as we could. My wife and I were very happy; we had a house outside the town, though I had to spend a great deal of time in Berlin. When I was sacked from Aachen, no one bothered to tell me. I was in Italy and read in the paper that Paul Van Kempen had been appointed as General Music Director in Aachen.[31]

RO Life had to go on and music was presumably as important to ordinary people trying to survive in Berlin as it was for the people who crowded into the National Gallery in London to hear Myra Hess's lunchtime recitals.

HvK I think many people nowadays have no conception of what it was like. We lived as best we could. I was lucky in that we were able to spend time away from Berlin. I knew the Swiss Ambassador, who had a country residence where it was possible to ride and relax. But the conditions in Berlin itself became worse and worse. In the end you had to try to put things that you saw out of your mind or else you would go mad.

RO You eventually managed to get a flight to Milan, where you stayed in hiding, and then you spent some time near Lake Como?

31 Paul Van Kempen (1893–1955), Dutch conductor. Dresden Philharmonic from 1935. As Karajan was too poorly established to be invited to Vienna where Baldur von Schirach was engaging Furtwängler, Knappertsbusch, Böhm, and R. Strauss for his national cultural showcase, his career slowly collapsed. In autumn 1942 he married the quarter-Jewish Anita Gütermann and applied to leave the Nazi Party which he had joined as a condition of the Aachen post in 1935. This was a *Nachgereichte* (NG) membership formally backdated to 1 May, 1933. A nomination made before the ban on the Party in June 1933 was never validated. Press comment on his early career is generally sensationalized and ill-informed.

HvK   We stayed hidden in a boat-house that was attached to a house of
people we knew. We had nothing at all to live on; but one day I
received a sum of money that we managed to divide up so that it
lasted for many weeks, just so much a day. Edwin Fischer had sent
it. It is a kindness I shall never forget.[32]

RO   You returned to Vienna via Trieste and your parents' home in
Salzburg; and then the real dramas began.

HvK   They had no idea. People were put into categories—high Nazis,
low Nazis—and subjected to endless cross-examination. I stayed
away. I said I would be happy to talk to anyone but I refused to be
subjected to personal attack. As far as restarting the musical life in
Vienna was concerned, we had the problem that the occupying
forces often contradicted each other. I was allowed to do one
concert[33] after being kept waiting most of the day by the Russians.
All they were interested in was striking deals to get hold of petrol,
which was in very short supply. I was with a player from the
Vienna Philharmonic who had been a Russian prisoner of war, so
he spoke some Russian. But it didn't get us very far. Eventually we
said, 'the people are already queuing outside the hall, the concert
starts in half an hour. Do we have it or not?' The man gave a
grunt, which was the permission we had been waiting for, and I ran
all the way back to my flat to change and conduct the concert.

RO   But that was something of a false dawn. They banned your next
concert.

HvK   Then Walter Legge turned up. He was English and he had been
very clever. He was only interested in making recordings and he

32   Edwin Fischer (1886–1960), Swiss pianist and conductor. Having lost most of his
possessions, including his library and his piano, in Berlin, Fischer set out on foot in 1942
to return to Switzerland, accompanied by his 80-year-old mother. Karajan still talked of
Fischer's help with evident emotion.

33   On 18 January 1946. The programme included a Haydn symphony, Strauss's *Don Juan*,
and Brahms's First Symphony. The recollections of the concert by the American cultural
officer in Vienna at the time, Henry Alter, are reprinted in the Haeusserman and
Vaughan biographies of Karajan: 'The hall was cold. People were wearing overcoats. The
Don Juan was incredible, the Brahms unforgettable.' Karajan later told Alter, 'If you
want me to stay for interrogation, you must first do something to prevent me from
starving.'

ROYAL FESTIVAL HALL
General Manager: T. E. Bean

PHILHARMONIA CONCERT SOCIETY

Artistic Director:
WALTER LEGGE

presents

PHILHARMONIA
ORCHESTRA
Leader: MANOUG PARIKIAN

HERBERT von KARAJAN

EDWIN FISCHER

PROGRAMME

BERLIOZ:	Symphonie Fantastique, Op. 14

INTERVAL

MOZART:	Piano Concerto No. 22 in E flat, K.482
MOUSSORGSKY-RAVEL:	"Tableaux d'une Exposition"

Friday, October 15th, 1954
at 8 p.m.

Management: IBBS & TILLETT LTD., 124 WIGMORE STREET, W.1

Karajan with Walter Legge

had a legal base in Switzerland, which also helped him avoid a lot of problems. We recorded Beethoven's Eighth Symphony in 1946. I think we used seventeen sessions. We found this again when we started recording the Beethoven symphonies with the Philharmonia Orchestra in London. Beethoven is very difficult because in the forte parts you don't have something to lean against; it's always that the strings play tremolo or very fast, which isn't really the basis for a sound. So again in London we spent nearly a week setting up the microphones and rehearsing.

RO   You managed to do some work in the preparation of the 1946 Salzburg Festival but there were still complications.

HvK   If it wasn't the Russians, it was the British who wanted to interfere; so I said, I am going away to wait for the day when once again an Austrian can decide when an Austrian may conduct music in his own country. I took a room in St Anton and spent six months with my ski instructor. He was also a man crazy about shooting. We spent a lot of time in the mountains. It was a time for being away from the cities, for reading[34] and reflection, and being alone with nature. When I eventually returned to Vienna to make music, I was completely relaxed within myself.

RO   By 1947–8 you were all more or less back in business— Furtwängler, Böhm, Knappertsbusch, and others. Erich Kleiber[35] also reappeared from South America. He has always had a high reputation in England and the Covent Garden Orchestra were obviously eager to work with him in the 1950s. But one very famous pianist—*not* a great destroyer of reputations—said to me recently, 'He was not a very nice man, and not as good as people said he was.'

---

34   One visitor found the floor of Karajan's room covered in theological books annotated in his 'seismograpic hand'. In a letter to Henry Alter, Karajan writes of his confidence being restored by the success of the 1946 Vienna recordings and of the period of seclusion and quiet concentrated meditation and study 'rediscovering myself in the vastness and solitude of the mountains'. See above, p. 8.

35   Erich Kleiber (1890–1956), Austrian conductor and father of Carlos Kleiber (b. 1930). Conducted first performance of Berg's *Wozzeck*, 1925. Teatro Colón, Buenos Aires, 1936–49.

Karajan with members of the Vienna Symphony Orchestra,
Vienna Westbahnhof, January 1950. When Furtwängler re-
established his hegemony in Salzburg, Berlin, and Vienna with
the Vienna Philharmonic in the late 1940s, Karajan gave
concerts with the unfashionable Vienna Symphony,
transforming it into a first-rate ensemble

HvK He was terrible! After the war there was much speculation in the newspapers and great headlines 'Kleiber is to return'. When he finally arrived, the directors of the State Opera, government ministers, and so on all put on their best clothes and went out to the airport to meet him. He held a press conference at the airport and was asked what he intended to do in Vienna. He replied, 'I have returned to cleanse the musical life of the city.' A friend showed me this in the newspaper. All I could say was, with what special materials does he propose to undertake this great task? Still, there was a lot of interest in his first concert. He had made a great reputation in Berlin between the wars. But I must say I was deeply disappointed. The theatre director Schuh[36] was there and he saw me sitting by myself during the interval. He was a man with a very impish wit. He came over and said, 'So I see you are not enjoying this concert. This comes as a great shock to me because it is well understood that anyone who does not like Erich Kleiber's conducting must be a Nazi!'

RO But what about his son, Carlos?

HvK I like him enormously, but he was also very much under the thumb of his father. He has come to discuss things with me on many occasions and I am always asking him to come and do just one concert with the orchestra. He has a genius for conducting but he doesn't enjoy doing it. He tells me, 'I conduct only when I am hungry.' And it is true. He has a deep-freeze. He fills it up, and cooks for himself, and when it gets down to a certain level then he thinks, 'now I might do a concert'. He is like a wolf! But he is someone I have the greatest admiration for.

RO When you came back down from the mountains you made some recordings that to this very day have a unique atmosphere about them—the *Metamorphosen*, the Brahms *Requiem*—but when you

---

36 Oscar Fritz Schuh (b. 1904), with designer Caspar Neher, oversaw Mozart productions in Salzburg from 1946, when he worked with the banned Karajan on a production of *Le nozze di Figaro* (cond. Prohaska). His principal collaborations were with Karl Böhm, though he also directed Mozart operas for Furtwängler, Gluck's *Orfeo ed Euridice* with Karajan in 1948, and the world première of Gottfried von Einem's *Dantons Tod*, Salzburg 1947, cond. Ferenc Fricsay. Schuh also directed a series of festival productions of plays by Eugene O'Neill.

went to England to work with Legge's Philharmonia there was an added interest to your music-making: the enormous repertory you managed to acquire and record.

HvK   Yes, I did many things which I have either forgotten or can't find time to return to now.

RO   Things like Roussel's Fourth Symphony.

HvK   No, I haven't forgotten that! I was very taken with the piece and at that time after the war the Lucerne Festival[37] was very interested in having the orchestra and allowing us to determine the repertory.

RO   It was in Lucerne that you conducted what were by all accounts electrifying performances of the Honegger *Symphonie liturgique*, which you later recorded for Deutsche Grammophon. It's a work that must have seemed to sum up the traumas of the war years and their aftermath for you?

HvK   I spent a great deal of time and study on it, over half a year, before I was ready to conduct it. It is a work that I could still come back to, perhaps.

RO   Legge really stabilized the Philharmonia's finances and was able to engage you permanently with the orchestra in 1949 as a result of money from the Maharaja of Mysore. Did you ever meet him?

HvK   No, but I was fascinated by this man because he wanted above all things for us to record the Bartók Music for *Strings, Percussion, and Celesta*. There was no recording at that time, and it was a very difficult piece for the orchestra to bring off but I was determined to do it. In a way, the very roots of music are touched on in this work.

RO   You say it was a difficult piece for the orchestra, but the Philharmonia was full of very gifted players.

37   As Lucerne was not in the grip of Allied administrators they were free to invite whoever they wished. Karajan was engaged in 1947. The Festival's loyalty to Karajan in 1947 has been amply repaid since.

HvK Very gifted, but in the early days the ensemble was not always very good. We had to work on it a great deal. And here I had the advantage of at least twenty years already in the profession. This you must have if players are going to accept that this or that is not right. And even then with a top orchestra there is more work to be done. In Vienna now Abbado is doing *Elektra*: over twenty orchestral rehearsals! Well, perhaps this is a few too many, but he knows after many years' experience that he can ask for this and that it is necessary.

2 · The Italian Connection

RO   You are regarded by many competent judges as one of the finest of all conductors of the music of Verdi and Puccini, which is a rare distinction for an Austrian- or German-born conductor. When did you first establish this Italian connection?

HvK   Bernhard Paumgartner[1] was my mentor in this as in so many other things. He took a great interest in young people, not only during the course of his duties at the Salzburg Mozarteum, but also beyond that. He took us on expeditions to Italy to see the architecture and the painting. He had a genius for explaining a work of art in a very few words. The language I studied much later, when I was waiting in Italy at the end of the war. I worked very hard. It kept me sane: that and the beauty of that particular Italian spring.

RO   And Italian opera? I imagine that in Austria, as in England at the time, it was rather frowned upon by so-called serious musicians?

HvK   When Toscanini brought *Lucia di Lammermoor* to Vienna with the La Scala Company, it was a revelation. I realized then that no music is vulgar unless the performance makes it so. When I was in Ulm, where the season ran only from September to April, I was able to travel a great deal; and then I went to Milan to hear real Italian singing. My training in Verdi's *Falstaff*[2] came from Toscanini. There wasn't a rehearsal in either Vienna or Salzburg at which I wasn't present. I think I heard about thirty. From

---

1 Bernhard Paumgartner (1887–1971), distinguished musicologist, conductor, composer, and academic administrator. His mother had been a singer at the Vienna Court Opera, his father a writer on music and a friend of Bruckner. Director of the Salzburg Mozarteum from 1917 to 1938 and again, after a period in Italy, from 1945 to 1959. Wrote and directed the music for Hofmannsthal's *Jedermann* at the first Salzburg Festival, 1920. In 1930 established a series of Salzburg Summer Conducting and Music Courses with which Karajan was involved. A programme of 22 July 1931 advertises the American pianist Frank Lawton in a concert with the Mozarteum Orchestra conducted by Herbert Karajan, consisting of the Overture to *Die Meistersinger*, the Schumann and Tchaikovsky B flat minor piano concertos, and Strauss's *Till Eulenspiegel.*.

2 Verdi's *Falstaff* has featured a good deal in Karajan's career. He has recorded it twice, for EMI in 1956 and for Philips in 1980. The EMI set, generally thought to be the better of the two, is something of a gramophone classic with a cast including Tito Gobbi, Rolando Panerai, and Elisabeth Schwarzkopf. Karajan's Vienna State Opera production was judged by Klemperer—an equivocal admirer—as being 'really excellent'.

Toscanini I learnt the phrasing, and the words—always with *Italian* singers, which was unheard of in Germany then. I don't think I ever opened the score. It was so in my ears, I just knew it.

R O Did Toscanini always command the best casts?

H v K In *Falstaff*, yes; but I remember a *Die Meistersinger* that was simply appalling, and a *Die Zauberflöte* . . . Not all his casts were good. He often seemed to have strange ideas about singers.

R O He wanted singers he could mould and dominate?

H v K No, I don't think it was that; it was simply the view he took of certain roles, certain music. Perhaps once it was personal. There is a story in La Scala that a very good singer once opened the door of a room where the maestro was preparing a lady for a little love-making, and he never worked for Toscanini again. But I remember also that Toscanini had a genius in choral work. At Bayreuth at that time the chorus was better at shouting than singing; they thought this was the true Wagner style. Toscanini put a stop to all that at his first rehearsal for *Tannhäuser*: 'No, no, nix Wagner, nix Bayreuth—*café chantant*!' He made a great effect by getting the chorus to sing a proper piano. When I opened my own season in Ulm with *Tannhäuser*, I had in my head an entirely new sound concept.

R O How did he get on with the pre-war Vienna Philharmonic?

H v K Generally well. There was a bass player in the orchestra who knew him and he told the orchestra, 'Toscanini is coming to conduct. We must do everything with the utmost precision, and beauty of tone. Please come half an hour before, sit down, and prepare. If we do this, it will be a success.' And it worked.[3]

R O But there was the famous walk-out when he stormed off the podium and then couldn't get out of the hall because all the doors were locked.

3 It would seem that Karajan gave the Philharmonia Orchestra similar advice when Toscanini came to conduct them in London in 1952. See Stephen J. Pettitt, *Philharmonia Orchestra: A Record of Achievement 1945–85* (London, 1985), 61.

HvK   And he went into the corner and cried. But it is necessary to tell the whole story. You know we have here in Austria a State Lottery. The players took the numbers in the score where Toscanini had lost his temper with them and entered them into the lottery. And they won a big prize—nowadays it would be the price of a family car. When Toscanini was told about this he *doubled* their winning for them. It is a wonderful story. If I had time I would like to make a collection of the many stories there are about great conductors because I think there is much to be learnt from them. You see, Toscanini was not a bad man; he was so musically dedicated and disciplined himself that he simply couldn't understand that some people can play a false note or play out of time. And perhaps, occasionally, he was frustrated by what he could or could not achieve. I always felt that he was never really happy with his performance of *La Mer*; he was searching for certain textures which he could never really get in hand.

RO   You met him?

HvK   Only once, after the war in La Scala, but he came to conduct the Philharmonia Orchestra in London and I prepared the orchestra for those concerts.[4] At the first rehearsal he played through the Brahms Second and changed nothing.

RO   Which other Italian conductors did you admire? I recall you speaking highly of Tullio Serafin?[5]

HvK   He was a good conductor, and a first-rate trainer of singers. But my real hero was Victor de Sabata.[6] I asked him once, 'What do

4   Toscanini paid close attention to the Philharmonia Orchestra's Italian tour of 1952. After a concert under Karajan at La Scala, Milan, on 20 May, Toscanini, at the age of 85, expressed interest in conducting the orchestra. The concerts, devoted to the four Brahms symphonies and the *Tragic Overture*, took place at the Royal Festival Hall on 29 September and 1 October 1952. Though six rehearsals were set aside for him, Toscanini was sufficiently impressed with the orchestra to use only four of them.

5   Tullio Serafin (1878–1968) conducted regularly at La Scala from 1909. Closely associated with Maria Callas's rise to prominence in the early 1950s, by which time Serafin was regarded as the doyen of Italian-born opera conductors.

6   Victor de Sabata (1892–1967), conductor and composer, son of a La Scala chorus-master and widely recognized as one of the most gifted, imaginative, and aurally sensitive conductors of his generation. Début at La Scala in February 1930 with Puccini's *La*

you feel when you conduct?' And he said, 'I have in my mind a million notes, and every one which is not perfect makes me mad.' He suffered in conducting. And that, I must say, I have passed. De Sabata was also probably the only person who never said one word against another conductor. He lived at a very difficult time; they wanted him back at La Scala, but there was always the possibility that Toscanini would return.[7]

RO John Culshaw tells of your listening to de Sabata's recording of *Tosca* and saying, 'No, he's right but I can't do it. That's *his* secret.'[8] Still, you've made two memorable recordings of *Tosca*.[9] It's a thrilling piece, but the characters are not exactly pleasant: Tosca, Scarpia . . .

HvK No, not at all pleasant. But *Tosca* has always fascinated me. Goethe once said: 'I would be able to commit all crimes in my life if I did not have the possibility to express them.' Sometimes you must conduct it, otherwise one day you may kill someone! I am fascinated by every single bar.

RO When did you first meet de Sabata?

HvK In Bayreuth in 1939. He was conducting *Tristan und Isolde*. At that time I was still on good terms with the General Intendant and he said, 'you should come to the rehearsals'. It was a revelation. The Isolde was Germaine Lubin[10]—gracious, noble, the most

fanciulla del West, followed shortly afterwards by a celebrated series of performances of Wagner's *Tristan und Isolde*. His 1953 EMI recording of Puccini's *Tosca* with Callas, Gobbi, and di Stefano is unsurpassed.

7 Though de Sabata conducted throughout the war in Italy, and occasionally in Germany, he was generally regarded as being a man oblivious of politics. According to the conductor Gianandrea Gavazzeni, 'He was so possessed by his musical demon that nothing else existed.' See Harvey Sachs, *Music in Fascist Italy* (London, 1987), 160–1.

8 John Culshaw, *Putting the Record Straight* (London, 1981), 301.

9 For RCA in Vienna in 1962 and for Deutsche Grammophon in Berlin in 1979.

10 Germaine Lubin (1890–1979), French soprano, studied at Paris Conservatoire and with Lilli Lehmann. Paris Opera 1914–44. Appeared at Bayreuth in 1938–9 as Kundry and Isolde. Recorded a good deal during the acoustic and early electrical period. 'Above all, she sang scrupulously: no whisking or wobbling, no lapse from lyrical standards even in the most strenuous passages of Brünnhilde's Immolation' (John Steane, *The Grand Tradition* (London, 1974), 238).

Karajan with his friend and mentor
Victor de Sabata, Milan, 1956

wonderful Isolde I have ever encountered, better than any of those endless German cannons who have sung the role. I remember also during that summer I thought it would be a nice idea to show Lubin some of the wonderful churches near Bayreuth. There are two in particular I thought she might like. She agreed to come and I took her first to the more brilliantly decorated one, not knowing that she was not only a very religious woman but also a girl who had been brought up in the strictest kind of convent—no heating, nothing for show. I can still remember proudly opening the door of the church and seeing the look of complete horror on her face. 'This is not a church,' she said. 'It is a boudoir!'

RO But that summons to Bayreuth in 1939 cost her dearly—the return to work in Paris, the accusations of collaboration, the suicide of her son.[11]

HvK I know. It was dreadful.

RO And Callas? I remember the English critic Philip Hope-Wallace saying that her Lucia with you in Berlin in 1955 robbed him of sleep for a week. And there are the recordings of *Madama Butterfly* and *Il trovatore* you made with her. She must have been a very extraordinary artist to work with?

HvK If she was handled rightly she was *very* easy. She was always prepared to the utmost and if she felt she had been given good advice, then she took it immediately. But she could sometimes be the diva. I remember I was once experimenting with a gauze—it had been in La Scala for a hundred years and was full of dust. She was short-sighted and could not see into the auditorium. She came to the rehearsal and came down the bridge over the orchestra where I was directing, and she said to the manager, 'If this veil remains, I do not sing.' So I let her just pass, and said, 'Oh, darling, I am looking for a new "element" . . .'; and after half an hour the manager came back to me and said that she was sitting upstairs

11 See the chapter on Lubin in Lanfranco Rasponi, *The Last Prima Donnas* (New York, 1975; London, 1984), 86–7, for her own account of events. Of Karajan and his second wife, Anita, she recalled, 'I saw a lot of the Karajans and can assure you that despite all that has been written, they were not Nazis.'

Maria Callas with Karajan and
members of the cast of the 1954
La Scala, Milan production of
Donizetti's *Lucia di Lammermoor*

weeping. So I said, 'Maria, I am experimenting and when I say "experiment" I mean I want to see how it presents itself. But I do not know if I will take it.' Of course, we took it, but then she saw the reason. But I would never want to upset anyone unless there was some very positive idea which we must try.

RO In her Juilliard classes,[12] she advised her pupils to work within the rubato available to the conductor. But she herself had a very remarkable rhythmic sense?

HvK Incredible. When she had a piece within her I said, 'Maria, you can turn away from me and sing, because I know you will never be one tiny part of a bar out.' She heard so well, and sang always with the orchestra.

RO It is frustrating that after the *Lucia* and the two EMI recordings there were no further productions with you both.

HvK I have to say that I regret deeply, deeply that I could not persuade her to make a film of *Tosca*. I told her that we already had the tape and that she would have nothing to do but be there and play the role. Onassis invited me—I didn't know him at the time but later we became great friends—and we talked. But then Maria began to get mad and she insisted on seeing everything beforehand. And Onassis said, 'I am rich, but I am not rich enough to pay for all this!' I continued to ask her. But she was afraid. She had left the thing and felt out of it.

RO The pirate recording of the Berlin *Lucia* has been a huge success on LP and even now on CD.

HvK I know about these pirate recordings and they cause a lot of trouble—this is something we have to be very careful about with our CD videos—but I know that sometimes there are things that we can never recapture and it is understandable that people will want to have them. I remember when some tapes were located of

12 Juilliard School of Music, New York, 1971–2, extracts released on record by EMI in 1987.

the last performance that Dinu Lipatti gave at Lucerne.[13] We all
knew he had only a few weeks left to live. He played Mozart's C
major Concerto, K467—a wonderful performance, so full of life
and beauty. The sound is poor but the spirit of the music is there.

RO   You talk about the fascination of *Tosca*. Another work you often
seem to have come back to is *Il trovatore*.

HvK   It is one of the first operas I conducted when I went to Ulm. As
I've said, I was always grateful to Verdi. With twenty-four players
and only four first violins, Verdi is still possible. Puccini is a
nightmare but Verdi is possible. Though later when I did the piece
in Vienna I was furious when the orchestra showed up with five
basses and a dozen first violins. For this music I must now have
sixteen first violins and eight basses. My conception of *Il trovatore*
is that here are what Jung called archetypes. Fear, hate, love—this
fascinates me. And, you know, there isn't one dull moment in the
entire opera!

RO   And you have recently returned to *Un ballo in maschera*, another
of your Ulm operas.[14] How well did you remember it?

HvK   When I played it through it came back to me completely, as things
do if you have really known them when you are young. So I knew
exactly why I wanted to conduct it. It has a special interest for me
because—just to take one aspect—it has an enormous number of
long ensembles: a bit like *Figaro*. When we were making the
recording I have to say it made me feel completely happy; it is a
piece which has such perfection of form. And we had a wonderful
cast.

RO   Domingo is your Riccardo. Where do you place him among the
tenors you have worked with?

13   On 23 August 1950, recently reissued on CD coupled with the recording of the
Schumann Piano Concerto Lipatti made with Karajan and the Philharmonia Orchestra in
1948, shortly before playing the work at Karajan's London début on 11 April in the
Royal Albert Hall.
14   Recorded for Deutsche Grammophon in Vienna, January 1989.

H v K He is for me the epitome of the Italian style at its best—he is Spanish, of course, but he has the true Italian style.

R O One of the Unitel films you have allowed Polygram to release is your Salzburg *Otello*, with Jon Vickers. It's an important historical document.

H v K I have long been fascinated by his work. He is a very complex man; he thinks deeply about every role and you must talk to him in great detail. But his presence on stage—above all, his delivery—is so good. In the great roles—his Tristan, his Otello—it seems to me he brings to the part a unique sense of musical phrasing. The phrasing may be very individual but he will lift it and project it. With so many singers the music simply goes in one particular way; with him it is always individual and special. Later in his career, when the top of the voice started to disappear, I tried to persuade him to do *Wozzeck* with me. He would have made a marvellous Wozzeck.

R O You recorded *Tristan und Isolde* with him; but you'd also directed Toscanini's Otello, Ramon Vinay, in the role in post-war Bayreuth.

H v K Yes, but Vickers was much better.

R O And José Carreras?

H v K If the crew was here I would play you the video of the Verdi Requiem. Did Caruso sing the 'Ingemisco' better, I wonder? He has had this terrible illness, but he is full of hope. From all that he has told me it was a terrible experience, but he has now set up his Foundation to help other sufferers, and this is a great joy to him. He is an adorable person, and as he is still young we all hope that he will make a new career now.

R O Of the Italian-born singers you worked with in the 1950s one thinks of Tito Gobbi in *Falstaff* and Rolando Panerai, who appeared on so many of your recordings—your Guglielmo in the famous *Così fan tutte*, di Luna in *Il trovatore*, and Ford on both your recordings of *Falstaff*.

Jon Vickers as Otello with Mirella
Freni as Desdemona in Karajan's
1970 Salzburg production of *Otello*

HvK Gobbi had sung Falstaff on many occasions. I remember him telling me how over the years it was a role which he had been able to approach from many different standpoints. Panerai, as you say, I worked with many times. He is a wonderful artist whom I've always admired. You know he's a farmer as much as a singer?

RO Like Verdi!

HvK No, he actually works the land. He has a man to do the finances, but he drives the tractors and so on. He has always impressed me as a man of great good humour, and with a wonderful fund of stories. I think he is one of the most balanced men I have ever met.

3 · Berlin Philharmonic

RO When did you first conduct the Berlin Philharmonic?

HvK My first concert was in 1938. I had been asked the previous year by the Intendant, Hans von Benda, in an arrangement they had for young conductors, but there was no rehearsal, so I declined. In 1938 I was offered a programme with full rehearsal and that I accepted, though when it came to the time I asked for separate section rehearsals—first strings, then winds—which met with some opposition, particularly as the orchestra was convinced that it knew the music already. But I loved the orchestra the moment I stood in front of it; and I knew from that moment that wherever my musical life might lead me in the meantime, this was what I wanted. This was where I could best express myself.

RO What was the programme?

HvK This I chose myself. It was Mozart's 'Haffner' Symphony, music from Ravel's *Daphnis et Chloé*, and the Brahms Fourth Symphony.[1]

RO Furtwängler died in November 1954 and you were offered the orchestra. Was it an uncomplicated succession?

HvK I said, 'I will give up everything for this orchestra, but in return I must ask that it be a lifetime's possession.' Too often I have seen the management of a city or of an orchestra decide, by some strange whim, 'Now we must have a change.' If I was to give my life to this orchestra then I could not allow that someone throw me out at a moment's notice.[2] The only practical problem at the time

1 Some sources record the Mozart symphony as No. 33 in B flat, K319. The concert was well received by critics, who appear to have been impressed by the fire and *élan* of the conducting, tempered by what was regarded at the time as a very 'modern' preoccupation with clarity of detail and overall form. This is well exemplified on the recording of Tchaikovsky's Sixth Symphony, 'Pathétique', which Karajan made with the orchestra in April 1939 and which has been reissued on CD as vol. 5 of Deutsche Grammophon's 'Herbert von Karajan: The First Recordings'.

2 The problems conductors can face with orchestral and municipal authorities are legion and a source of continuing instability that makes it increasingly difficult for productive, long-term relationships to establish themselves. Though Karajan terminated his life contract with the Berlin Philharmonic on 24 April 1989, citing health problems and the continuing failure of the Berlin Senate to define his duties and rights, the artistic achievements of the 'contract for life' that lasted for over thirty years are there for all to recognize.

Karajan at the time of his début
with the Berlin Philharmonic in 1938

was that I would have to take the orchestra on its American tour in the first months of 1955 at a time when I was contracted to conduct a new *Ring* cycle at La Scala, Milan. I said to the manager, Ghiringhelli, who was already a great personal friend, that it was important for me to go, but if it was not possible then I would forget it. He was very, very kind; he said of course I must go with the orchestra. From that time I had a wall to lean my back on.

RO   The American tour wasn't especially easy, I gather. Anti-German feelings were still running high.

HvK   I remember getting off the plane and being asked by the press photographers if I would give them a salute. So I raised my arm and gave them a very big thumbs-down. The bigger problem for me at the time was the way the orchestra was playing. In Vancouver we began with a Beethoven overture, and the first chord—it was like picking up a sponge, there was no body in the tone. I would have liked to creep to the edge of the podium and disappear. So I said, we must do some basic things. How to play a fermata with full tone. They thought I meant for five seconds but I made them practise holding their tone for twenty or thirty seconds.

RO   The recent Beethoven Fifth Symphony in Berlin[3] had massively sustained tone in the fermatas but with no loss of forward impetus in the playing.

HvK   I know, but we worked very hard on that. They became very impatient with me!

RO   You presumably had to work on the orchestra section by section. I notice from the old schedules that you programmed Vaughan Williams's *Fantasia on a Theme by Thomas Tallis* a good deal at that time.[4] Was this a way of working on the quality of the strings?

HvK   No, it was a piece I am very fond of and it happened to be in quite a few programmes at that time. My plans had to be very long-term at first. In the first place, we had to come to know each other, to

3   December 1988.
4   Karajan recorded it with the Philharmonia Orchestra in 1953.

establish a community of interest, and so we used the early tours and concert schedules to play through the orchestra's main repertory. Also, I knew exactly where the orchestra's deficiencies were. Many players, as it happened, were coming near to the age of retirement, so it was possible over a period of six or seven years to make the orchestra young again.[5] From the first, I asked that every member of the orchestra must have within himself great musicianship and great culture. So we had to search quite a time to find these players. At first I could not devote so much time to the orchestra but by the early 1960s I was coming to a position where I was able to be with the orchestra a very great deal, working for eight or ten days at a time on concerts, records, and films.

RO   But we are looking not just at the renewing of an orchestra over one decade but a process of change and evolution over more than three decades.

HvK   This made it a greater challenge later on. Beecham said that any fool can conduct three concerts with an orchestra, but to go on improving is like going on a race track where it is possible to improve your time at first, but each new improvement involves great effort and often some danger. In the Berlin orchestra we always looked for greater knowledge and better players but maintaining standards is always going to be difficult.

RO   Many organizations rely simply on good talent-spotting, but you set up an array of musical foundations, some of which are still operative.

HvK   I had the idea for a school in Berlin that would help train the musicians we would need in the future. As always, we had the idea but not the money! Then we gave a concert for the 100th anniversary of the Dresden Bank. The head of the bank was Jürgen Ponto—who was so tragically assassinated—a man with an enormous love of music. He came to me and said, 'I have talked with my directors and they will give you from now on DM 250,000 a year.' He believed that our problem was one that faces

5   In 1977, Karajan told me there were just six players left from the orchestra that had toured America with him in 1955.

Karajan rehearsing the
Berlin Philharmonic in 1955

many great enterprises today and he believed that by helping us, who are seen and heard in so many places, he and his bank were making a contribution to our cultural life.

RO How was the school to be organized?

HvK The idea was quite clear. Our soloists in the orchestra would be professors. The upper age limit for entrants was set at 25, the lower limit we didn't set. Race, religion, nationality, Prix de Rome: all ignored. We are interested only in quality. Someone once said to me, 'You are surely not founding an élitist system?'—that's a word that seems very unfashionable these days. I said, 'No, my system is not élitist; it is super-élitist.' All I say is, if someone cannot play in rhythm and has not music within him, then we cannot admit him.

RO You were supplementing rather than competing with other musical institutions and also indirectly benefiting other orchestras?

HvK For many things they can go to the Hochschule für Musik. And, yes, we have not been able to employ them straight away, though they could come into the orchestra to sit with the principals as a co-pilot sits with the pilot. If they come from the Berlin orchestra, they need no references, so other orchestras will take them; though we know that one day they will return to this orchestra.

RO Players obviously come and go; not everyone stays until the retiring age.

HvK It is important that an orchestra has new young players coming in all the time—we recently had a young Polish violinist who is one of the orchestra's concert-masters, he is *very* promising, and full of music[6]—but sometimes players leave us to fulfil their own dreams and ambitions. One of our violinists left us to start his own violin school, and also a flying school. He has his independence and he tells me he has never been happier in his life. Sometimes it is a problem if a player goes, for whatever reason. I missed very much the man who was for fifteen years our first trombone; he trained the group to the very highest level.

6 Daniel Stabrawa.

RO   People notice the leader of an orchestra but often forget the importance of the section heads.

HvK   In Vienna there is a man called Schulz, who is a kind of genius. He doesn't always play. I once specially asked for him to be there and then demanded to know at the rehearsal who was this man sitting with the flutes. 'It is Schulz,' they said. 'You asked specially for him!' The thing about this man is that the whole wind section seems to play better when he is there, not just the flutes. In Vienna there is also the concert-master Hetzel, who is someone I really value. He watches me the whole time. I sometimes worried that he didn't have enough time to see his own music but it seems he has it by memory. I have also been lucky in Berlin. My first leader was Schwalbé, who had been with the Suisse Romande under Ansermet, and now they have Spierer, who is a good musician and totally reliable. He suffered a great personal tragedy two years ago but he remains with the orchestra. He is a man for whom I have the greatest admiration.

RO   The old Philharmonia Orchestra wasn't short of major talent— Dennis Brain, for instance.

HvK   He was a wonderful player but it was not so much the true German sound. My ideal here is Seifert, who is quite simply the best horn player in the world.

RO   I remember Menuhin writing that Karajan protects his musicians, sees they are well paid, ensures the quality of their instruments, encourages them to play chamber music, and generally boosts their morale . . .[7]

HvK   I have always been interested in educating an orchestra from the musical point of view and at the level of human contact. If they are ill they get good doctors, if there is a divorce . . . over the years we

7   Yehudi Menuhin, *Unfinished Journey* (London, 1976), 315. Menuhin wrote: 'Karajan follows a long line of great conductors, but he is more than a conductor, he is a leader of men.' Karajan talks of accompanying Menuhin in Beethoven or Mozart as one accompanies a great singer. When Menuhin turned seriously to conducting, he worked with Karajan who, in turn, invited Menuhin to conduct a regular series of pre-Christmas concerts in Berlin.

Karajan in performance

have worked and experimented to discover new things and remember old ones. It is important never to fall into routine; and it is important that when we make music the audience *sees* that we enjoy playing well. But this cannot survive if an orchestra loses its individuality and independence. There is talk now of the German orchestras working to new contracts. This would lay down specifically when they can and cannot play or rehearse. If they sign it, it will ruin them.

RO   Thinking of, for example, those summer vacation sessions[8] you used to have with the Berlin players in Saint-Moritz in the 1960s and '70s, I am sure one day people are going to be looking back to all this as some great Golden Age that has now gone for good.

HvK   In Saint-Moritz we were able to do things we couldn't possibly arrange during the season. We would often decide what to play on the spur of the moment. If the weather was fine and we wanted to be out in the mountains, then we would only work in the evening. If it was wet, we might spend the day making music. It was a very good atmosphere for music-making.

RO   Who was invited? The recordings you made were mainly smaller-scale pieces.

HvK   The best players; but with so many good players we could alternate the groups so that no one felt they had been left out.

RO   This was chamber music-making, but still with the full and characteristic Berlin sound?

HvK   In the sense that every note is given its full length and value, this is true. We know how thrilled Mozart was when he had more and better string players to realize his music. Perhaps this is now an

---

8 Between 1964 and 1972 Karajan made a considerable number of recordings on vacation with the Berliners at the tiny French Protestant church in Bad Saint-Moritz. The repertoire consisted mainly of music by Bach, Vivaldi, and Handel, with some Mozart divertimentos and early symphonies, Haydn's 'Hen' Symphony, and Rossini string sonatas. But Karajan also used the occasions to record Honegger's Second Symphony, Stravinsky's *Apollo*, and Strauss's *Metamorphosen*, the 1969 Deutsche Grammophon recording.

old-fashioned view; but posterity can judge what is good music-making and what are merely the trends of a particular time.

RO It seems now that we are living in an era of endless chopping and changing of conductors and orchestras, with increasingly few lengthy tenures—in the West at least.

HvK This is why I advised Masur to keep what he has. In many ways they do not have the resources we have in the West, but in Leipzig Masur has a pool of well over 200 musicians whom he has trained up very well. He is an excellent musician and a great enthusiast. They will now come and do the concerts for the Salzburg Easter Festival.

RO You have had good relations with the Dresden orchestra, too. For many people your 1974 Dresden recording of Wagner's *Die Meistersinger* is one of the most congenial and profound of all your recordings.

HvK It was a congenial occasion! Suddenly I fell in love with that piece all over again, and also I think the Dresden orchestra was determined to prove that it was a truly great orchestra—which it is.[9] And they know that music so well. And yet despite that they insisted on two full public play-throughs with one of my assistants before the sessions started.

RO Did you ever conduct the Leningrad Philharmonic, the orchestra Mravinsky[10] had for fifty years?

HvK I would have gladly done so, if I had had time. But they always said that I must bring my own orchestra.

RO I heard once that you wanted to conduct Shostakovich's Sixth Symphony but you thought Mravinsky had done it so well you wouldn't touch it.

9 At the end of the *Meistersinger* sessions Karajan said: 'My agent in Berlin once said to me: "Wait until you stand in front of the Dresden Staatskapelle. Their playing shines like old gold." A great deal of the city has been destroyed but you have remained a living monument to Dresden's tradition and culture.'

10 Evgeny Mravinsky (1903–88) was Chief Conductor of the Leningrad Philharmonic from 1938 onwards.

HvK   Yes, I did. I was a great admirer of his conducting. He was the representative of this older generation in perfection.

RO   And Szell?[11] His achievement in Cleveland was not dissimilar to yours in Berlin and Mravinsky's in Leningrad?

HvK   Szell and I were great friends. I remember, he was always insisting that I conduct the Prokofiev Fifth. I wondered what he wanted, so I did it; and in the interval of the rehearsal he came and said he was suffering from nervous shock because the moment I started he realized I was doing exactly the contrary of all the things he had taught the orchestra. It seemed like a complete breakdown; but after a few minutes he saw that they were playing as if they had always played this way. And, as you know, there is a passage with the cellos at the start of the finale of this symphony that is quite crucial. In the interval of *my* concert, he took the cellos away to ensure that the passage was perfect when we came back to play it— now *there* is real dedication and real generosity!

RO   Klemperer once said that Szell was a machine, but a very good machine.

HvK   No, you cannot really say that. He was a man with a full heart. When you had a chance to meet him in his house with his guests, he was a most charming and intelligent man. No, I can't understand that remark.

RO   What about the Cleveland Orchestra now?

HvK   I hear very good things of Christoph von Dohnányi. He comes from a very distinguished family, of course, with a tragic history. The Nazis shot his father, you know, and his uncle, the theologian Bonhoeffer. He is a good musician, intelligent, with a wide range of interests. I think the orchestra is in good hands.

RO   What about concert halls? You've conducted all over the world, including one place in India where you told the orchestra to play forte throughout in order to defeat the noise of the

11   George Szell (1897–1970), Hungarian conductor, permanent conductor of the Cleveland Orchestra from 1946 onwards.

air-conditioning, the Vatican, and the great open-air theatre at Epidaurus in Greece.

HvK I conducted the Verdi Requiem at Epidaurus. It is a magnificent setting but I don't like playing music in the open air, and the acoustics there are not perhaps as good as they are claimed to be. The Vatican, I must say, is not too bad when it is full and the resonance is reduced. My ideal is the Philharmonie in Berlin.[12] Before it was built we were very much under stress, because the church where we recorded was on a flight-path into Berlin, so we sometimes had to stop and re-record a passage five or six times before we got it right.

RO The Philharmonie hasn't been without its critics.

HvK I have to admit that at first it wasn't completely right. It was a basically good design which needed further improvements to it. There was also a lot of resistance to moving from the church to a new permanent home. The people who moved the instruments each day to the studio had a vested interest in persuading us that the Philharmonie was no good; people even said privately that the change must be resisted at all costs because the coffee was so much better at the church! We were greatly helped soon after the opening of the Philharmonie when Jochum[13] came to conduct a concert. He made a public pronouncement that the Philharmonie was impossible to record in. This was not true—he was very much a dilettante in these things—but it shocked people into making the changes we needed. Later, a great step came when we started making films. We had to change the design of the orchestra's stage seating so that the cameras could get the proper angles on the

12 Designed by Hans Scharoun and inaugurated in the autumn of 1963. It seats approximately 2,200 'in terraces on different levels which slope, like vineyard-covered hillsides, and are grouped around the orchestral podium as around an arena'. Karajan has conducted in all four Berlin Philharmonic halls: the old Philharmonie, the Titania Palace, the concert-hall of the Music Academy, and the new Philharmonie.

13 Eugen Jochum (1902–87) is best remembered for his Bruckner interpretations, some of which were recorded with the Berlin Philharmonic. His flexible tempi and fondness for Nowak editions of the Bruckner symphonies put him in a different category from Karajan as a Bruckner interpreter.

players, and the new wooden structure made a great difference to the sound we were able to get in the hall. These things all took time but now I must say that, for me, it is just about perfect.

4 · On Conducting

RO When we were watching the end of the film of Brahms's First Symphony which you've been editing, I noticed you giving a very accurate two-handed performance of the timpani part on the table in front of you.

HvK It is the one orchestral instrument that I learned to play when I was young.[1]

RO Quite a few leading conductors have started life as orchestral players: Münch and Kempe were in the same orchestra, the Leipzig Gewandhaus, at the same time. How important is first-hand orchestral experience for a conductor?

HvK It depends on the circumstances. In Ulm—as in many other opera-houses years ago—it was vital that the conductor was a good pianist because he was not only conductor but also chorus-master and principal *répétiteur*. But it is also necessary to know music-making from the orchestra's point of view. In Ulm I shared the conducting with a man called Otto Schulmann. When he was conducting I would often sit in the orchestra in the middle of the woodwinds. I learnt a lot from this. In practical terms, no one can learn every orchestral instrument. If you tried, you would be dead before you had finished the training. And even if you were, for instance, a good violinist you would never be as good as your best players. The important thing for the conductor is that he must learn what it is possible to *ask* for.[2]

RO To an extent, of course, the orchestra is the instrument the conductor is himself trying to master.

1 Simon Rattle is another example of a timpanist who became a conductor. Though Rattle attended a Karajan rehearsal in Berlin, and Karajan's October 1988 London concert, both men, it seems, were too shy to make further contact. Rattle's long-term dedication to a single orchestra is something Karajan spoke of with approval.

2 How a conductor can usefully guide a skilled instrumentalist has been illustrated by the violinist and Karajan protégée Anne-Sophie Mutter. In an interview with Reinhard Beuth, *Encounter*, 70 (May 1988), 71, she noted: 'Karajan has a phenomenal knack of judging things from the outside. He's not a violinist, nor is he capable of thinking like a violinist; things like fingering and bow changes he's not interested in at all . . . The result is that he has ideas about phrasing that you might have as a singer, say, but not as a violinist because you are too close to the actual material, too wrapped up in technique.'

HvK   This is true, and no one can say they know a score, however well it
may be known in the mind, until it has been tried on the orchestra.
The moment you stand in front of an orchestra you hurt yourself
on the inertia of the matter. I am not talking here about laziness.
To create a sound involves a huge corporate effort. Why do we
have rehearsals? The conductor will say, 'So that I can
communicate my ideas to the orchestra'; and the orchestra will say,
'So that he can learn the repertory at our expense'; and the manager
will say, 'Because I am paying for all this and I insist you rehearse.'
But there is a sense in which a rehearsal is the process of coming to
terms with a great resistance. We know that Michelangelo regarded
the marble he worked in as his own personal enemy. And we know
the experience of pianists working at the keyboard. Gieseking[3] once
told me that he was given a new short piece to learn. It was about
ten minutes long and he had before him a two-hour train journey.
He had a marvellous memory; so he learnt, and went to the hall
and played it. But then, he said, the shock came. The moment you
come to play, the moment when you feel the pressure of the whole
body on the keys—that is when the real process of interpretation
really begins. And so it is with the orchestra. They learn from me,
and I also learn a great deal from them. And only when I have
experienced this pressure, through them, and absorbed it, can I feel
that here is the beginning of an interpretation.

RO   Like so much else in music, this is a process that involves the
passage of a lot of time: learning a work on the page and then on
the orchestra?

HvK   It will certainly take a great deal of time. And this is why your first
attempt to conduct a great work will often end up as a disaster,
because you don't know where the real points of stress are, you
don't know how the piece is distributed. In this, experience helps
enormously. When you conduct a symphony for the first time you
may fear a breakdown in every bar. But if you know the thing, you
know where to apply the concentration. It is the same with a great
surgeon. He knows where nothing can go wrong, where the young

3   Walter Gieseking (1895–1956), German pianist famous for his interpretations of Mozart
and Debussy. He made several recordings with Karajan in the early 1950s for EMI.

Karajan studying at his home in Saint-Moritz. Walter Legge noted: 'He is one of the few conductors I have known who has never made a mark in a score. He will absorb a score quietly sitting on the floor, like a relaxed Siamese cat. Over the years he has learned how completely to relax the body so the mind is absolutely free to do what it wants.'

man is worrying 'My God, if something happens which I have not calculated for. . .'. And so the experienced surgeon is able to apply his real concentration at the decisive moment. And this is also how you reserve your energies. Many younger conductors are more exhausted after a concert than I am now. Nowadays *Tristan und Isolde* would not especially exhaust me. But the first time I conducted it I needed an ambulance to take me home!

RO   So the young maestro in intensive care may not have conducted a very effective *Tristan* or Beethoven Seventh?

HvK   No, because in the case of the Beethoven Seventh, he may not have learnt that quick music sounds dull unless every note is articulated. The last movement of this symphony is certainly a case in point. When I was a young conductor in Germany it was usual to conduct the finale much slower than we hear it nowadays. And I knew it was wrong, but I couldn't get out of this tradition because of the difficulty of realizing the inner content of the music. It did not—how can I put it?—lend itself to a faster tempo. Then, eventually, both things were joined: the right tempo and the content. Sometimes, especially in Romantic music, I tell the orchestra, 'Now play everything as you played it but play a 4/4 bar. What you are doing is feeling the music so deeply that you are playing a 5/4 bar. So feel with the same intensity but do the contrary.'

RO   You have always had a passion for rhythmic accuracy and long-term rhythmic control.

HvK   This is the one thing that might make me lose my temper. I can accept a wrong note from an orchestra but when everything is getting faster or slower, that I cannot accept. In this matter many teachers should be arrested for misleading the young! This is one of the reasons why I set up my Foundations. I wanted to give back something for the great interest and happiness I have had from being able to make music to people. But I said, 'what can I do?' And here it seems to me that music education is one of the most neglected things in our culture today. And if pupils are not taught the basic disciplines of rhythm—then things become impossible.

RO You had yourself computer-tested once?

HvK That was in Dortmund at the scientific institute there. They have a piano—not a very good one!—which is connected to a computer. It measures the distance between notes. At the change-over of the third finger and thumb, for instance, some pianists seem to get quicker, others slower. But what they did to me was give me a metronome and a theme which you play in quicker and quicker note values: triplets, eighths, sixteenths, and so on. I know that orchestras, when they see a lot of black notes, usually start to accelerate. I made, I think, a 2 per cent or 3 per cent error over the whole test. So they said, 'Herr von Karajan apparently has a computer in his brain!' But it is not a computer. I trained it, with metronomes. And I still test myself. I can walk in 120 and sing in 105; and if you ask me to sing in 105 now, I will manage it. If I get it wrong, I feel it with my whole body. And in the orchestra, if a solo comes in slower or faster, I sense it right away; it makes me feel uneasy.

RO Is this why your Bruckner is so formidable? In something like the Adagio of the Eighth Symphony we intuitively experience an overall stability, a kind of musical wholeness.

HvK Yes, but this comes, too, from an overall knowledge of the work. If you can feel and see the whole work laid out before you as you begin, then this will be achieved. Also, the tempi in the original Bruckner scores are much simpler than they come to be in some editions.[4] Bruckner often wants a slight modification of tempo and he writes 'langsamer'; but sometimes people drop to about 30 per cent of the tempo! No, it is much subtler than this—like the Viennese waltz. No one has ever tried to edit a Viennese waltz: all those inflexions of tempo would look terrible on the page. Only lately, though, have I been able to get virtually one pulse through the entire work. It takes years to achieve this.

RO In general, you have followed the Bruckner editions edited by Robert Haas. Did you know him?

4 Those edited by Leopold Nowak.

HvK   Yes, I knew both Haas and Nowak.[5] Haas was a very great editor
and made important restorations; but you can't always go back to
Bruckner's first ideas—the first version of the Eighth Symphony,
for example, where the first movement ends with a fortissimo coda.

RO   Josef and the man you knew, Franz Schalk, had made some fairly
horrendous alterations to Bruckner's scores.

HvK   I think they had good intentions. The symphonies are full of
difficulties and in those days the orchestras had not always the
resources we have today. If Bruckner calls for eight horns with
some of the players playing also the tenor and bass tubas, this can
cause a great strain. Now I might have extra players so that there
can be some moments of rest for the players in one of the very
long symphonies; but in Bruckner's day it was often a matter of re-
scoring a passage because you knew that the third horn was not a
very good player and that is all you had.

RO   You must have known people who remembered Bruckner—
Paumgartner's father had known him, Schalk . . .

HvK   My father remembered very well Bruckner concerts. He heard the
Bruckner Te Deum. During the performance the audience left bit
by bit, banging the doors behind them. About half the audience
had gone by the interval and by the end he was virtually alone. But
Bruckner's music is primordial. Perhaps you have to go to the
church at St Florian[6] to understand why the music is as it is, with
so many pauses and such great spaciousness.

5   Robert Haas (1886–1960), Austrian musicologist and pioneering first editor of the
Bruckner Critical Edition. Head of music section of the Austrian National Library,
Vienna, from 1920 to 1945, when he was replaced by Leopold Nowak, who also took
over the direction of the Bruckner Edition. The decision to replace Haas in a job he had
carried out for a quarter of a century with a mixture of wisdom and devotion was largely
political. This was a further example, Karajan suggested, of a man's political affiliations
being wrongly interpreted and used against him.

6   The famous baroque church of the Augustinian monastery near Linz. Bruckner was born
in nearby Ansfelden and was closely connected with the monastery from his earliest
years. By special dispensation, his coffin was placed beneath the great organ of the
church.

RO Is it true you were once locked into the vault under the church with Bruckner's coffin?

HvK No, no, not locked! But I was taken to the vault before a concert in the church. It was during the war when the convent had been turned into a shrine for Bruckner by a man called Glasmeier.[7] The idea was that I should be in the right state of mind for the concert I was about to conduct.

RO Bruno Walter once said that there is in every great work only one real climax. Would you agree?

HvK Certainly.

RO Yet the other day I was listening to an eminent conductor whose Bruckner is often much praised reaching a triple forte long before what is to me self-evidently the work's pivotal climax.

HvK But, you see, this is a most interesting fact that you have noticed. So many conductors—and I must say Furtwängler was sometimes one of these—create enormous crescendi; and after them the music collapses. It is like a man who storms up to the top of a great mountain and then just drops down. And this was Bruno Walter's great point. When you are up then you must *know* that you are up! You enjoy the view and you are stimulated by it.[8] Also the end must feel as though it is an end. This is true of Bruckner, where codas can become slower and slower. I say to the orchestra, this is not the way; you must think of the last bars as a fermata, a fermata that lasts the entire length of the coda. We sustain the metronome. If we do not, the book has no proper end.[9]

7 Heinrich Glasmeier, former First World War cavalry officer, music-lover, and entrepreneur, who as Head of German Radio commandeered St Florian for lavish wartime Bruckner festivals.

8 With Karajan this is no idle analogy. A mountain-man all his life, he succeeded at the age of 57 in making a twenty-two hour ascent of Mont Blanc after which, accompanied by three guides, he ski'd back in a remarkable twenty-seven minutes of skiing time.

9 When Karajan conducted a performance of Bruckner's Seventh Symphony with the Vienna Philharmonic in London on 5 April 1962, the critic of the *Daily Telegraph*, Donald Mitchell, wrote of the performance of the slow movement: 'Karajan built the movement up to its final climax with consummate art. But it was not, perhaps, in the famous and glorious burst of C major affirmation that he was at his most impressive. It

RO   You mentioned earlier walking in one tempo and singing in another. Walking pace often seems to give us the pulse of a movement; and walking pace and heartbeat are often linked.

HvK   This is very usual and enormously important. Different conductors have different pulse rates and their tempi are often mathematical proportions of this. Bach's music is almost always at the pulse of a heartbeat. Again, I know this from my long experience of yoga. I know what my heartbeat is: I feel it in every part of me. And if I fall into the pulse at the start of a piece of music it is a physical joy. In this way, your whole body makes music. This is why I was so concerned when we were making the new set of the Beethoven symphonies in 1977. After the recordings we had mixing sessions. I took some tapes with me to Saint-Moritz and listened, and thought, my goodness, this is quite wrong. Then I realized. In Saint-Moritz you are higher, and your heartbeat is faster. It felt wrong to me, but only there.

RO   You are against beating metronomically.

HvK   Absolutely. What you should know is how much tempo passes *overall* in one certain phrase, and this is the most important thing.

RO   What about metronome markings in, say, Beethoven?

HvK   Naturally one examines them—some are good, others, perhaps in the Ninth Symphony, involve mistakes. But it comes back to the point of how much tempo passes in the one phrase. We don't know how Beethoven conducted his music or how he would have conducted if he had been able to hear everything that was going on, but we know from Brahms's letters that he allowed himself sometimes great flexibility. You remember that von Bülow[10]

was in his wonderfully sensitive treatment of the movement's quiet coda that he revealed his full stature as a conductor. This was a moment undoubtedly touched by interpretative genius.'

10   Hans von Bülow (1830–94), German pianist and conductor. Gave first performances of *Tristan und Isolde* and *Die Meistersinger* as well as Brahms's Fourth Symphony. Richard Strauss succeeded von Bülow as principal conductor in Meiningen in 1885 and two years later von Bülow became the first permanent conductor of the Berlin Philharmonic Orchestra.

prepared the first performances of the Fourth Symphony with the Meiningen Orchestra but that Brahms himself accompanied and conducted the German tour. And at that time he wrote in a letter, 'In these concerts I couldn't make enough slowings and accelerations.'[11]

RO So it is a combination of a stable inner pulse and flexibility of response within that. You talked earlier about the inertia of the orchestral mass and the physical strain there is on both the conductor and the players. This is something you have instituted scientific research into through one of the Karajan foundations?

HvK Yes, we set up a unit affiliated to the University of Salzburg to look into the question of stress in music-making; and also the influence of music on the mind and the body, of healthy people and sick people. I have a slow heartbeat, about 67 or 68, but we found that in a quiet passage of music before a climax the heartbeat could rise to 170. Slow music with intermittent pauses puts the greatest stress on the system, both on the mind and on the body. And we know that this can cause damaging, even fatal, stress.[12]

RO Again, I have seen it said: this is all very interesting but it is hardly new.

HvK And as a result of the dilettante attitude you describe men have died: three of my colleagues, two at virtually the same place in Act III of *Tristan*.

RO How do you dissipate this enormous tension?

HvK In a passage of great internal stress I will breathe very freely.

---

11 'Ich kann mir in dem Fall oft nicht genug tun mit Treiben und Halten . . .'. Karajan is quoting the letter Brahms wrote to Joseph Joachim in Vienna, 20 January 1886 (*Johannes Brahms im Briefwechsel mit Joseph Joachim*, ed. A.Moser (Berlin, 1908), ii. 205). Brahms is referring specifically to the difficulty of obtaining fully expressive performances of new or unfamiliar music. Once the music was in 'the flesh and blood' of the musicians, he advocated less extreme measures. The Berlin Philharmonic has had Brahms's music in its flesh and blood for over a hundred years and remains unparalleled as a Brahms orchestra.

12 The most famous recent case was Karajan's exact contemporary, Joseph Keilberth (b. 19 April 1908), who died whilst conducting a performance of *Tristan und Isolde* in Munich on 21 July 1968.

RO Orchestral players themselves don't necessarily lead the healthiest lives!

HvK And yet they are under enormous stress when they are doing their best work. An orchestral player works as hard as a navvy. Which is why I have always tried to insist that my players have proper ways of relaxing away from their work.

RO I notice that even when you are simply listening to music on tape or watching it on the TV monitor when you are editing you are still breathing with the music even though you are not conducting it. Does this all come from your long training in yoga?

HvK Yes, in the language of Buddhism you do not speak about 'How I impel this thing' but how it releases itself. I have often referred to my own fear when I was first required to make a horse jump a fence. I was told: 'Set the right angle and then leave it, do not disturb it.'

RO And setting the right angle comes in rehearsal?

HvK For good rehearsing you need a mind like a microscope. It is not a personal matter. You are not helping the players, because if you try to do that they will come to rely on you in the actual performance. In rehearsal it is a matter of establishing the correct way to play the notes. But in the performance it is a totally different thing. There is a sense in which the greatest art in conducting is to know when one should not conduct.

RO In performance you often appear to be in a state of deep meditation.

HvK Well, I have practised yoga for many years, but then I met a Jesuit priest who had been sent to the Far East by the Catholic Church to experience the Buddhist way and see how it might relate to Catholic worship. He came to two of my concerts and afterwards we had a long talk. He said the traditional exercises I was doing were unimportant in comparison with the meditative disciplines I was experiencing whilst making music.

RO Ideally, you become one with the piece itself?

HvK Do you know the story of the buffalo? One day a young man went to the guru to seek his help. The guru sent him into his hut—just a small, leaf-covered hut with a narrow door—to meditate on his parents. The young man came out again. He couldn't concentrate. The guru suggested he meditate on a rose. Again, failure. So the guru asked him: 'What is the thing that is dearest to you?' And the young man said it was a buffalo that lived on his farm. 'So, go into my hut and meditate on that', said the guru. After a very long time the young man had not reappeared. Eventually the guru was so worried he called into the hut to see what was happening. The young man said he was fine. 'So why do you not come out?' asked the guru. 'I have the problem', the young man replied, 'that I cannot manoeuvre my horns through your narrow door.' 'Now you have reached the first stage', said the guru. It is a nice story!

RO You have the score in your mind—you once said you don't need a tape or a score to oversee in your mind the whole of *Tristan*—and this has obviously been true of other great conductors. But you also use the time you have with your orchestra to help them approach this state, too.

HvK There is a problem here with the eyes, with the musician being chained to the printed page in front of him. I remember during some very intensive rehearsals we were doing for the *Ring* we came to a passage where the figuration of the accompaniment always comes out too strongly. I said, 'Gentlemen, this will never be right until you have mastered it completely and are free of the page. When we have achieved that, then you will be able to play, not looking at the page all the time, but hearing the woodwinds, which have the melody at this point.' There can also be problems with the way the music is printed. Sometimes it is possible to trace some problems with tempo or balance to the parts the musicians are using.

RO All this explains your long-standing fondness for conducting with closed eyes.[13]

13 'His eyes shut, Karajan projects the image he has perceived internally' (Robert Oboussier, *Deutsche allgemeine Zeitung*, 9 Apr. 1938).

Karajan with the designer of his Salzburg Festival *Ring* cycle, Günther
Schneider-Siemssen (*back to camera*), with Wieland Wagner and
Walter Legge during the 1962 Bayreuth Festival. Though Karajan's
own work took him away from Bayreuth after the famous 1952
production of *Tristan und Isolde*, the influence of Wieland Wagner on
his theatre work remained very much in evidence

HvK It can help you concentrate on the inner content of the music; and I have always been able to establish a real sense of what the musicians are doing. It is a kind of intuition.

RO Recently, though, and certainly on some of the films, you seem to be conducting more with the eyes open.

HvK Sometimes it is a matter of establishing a direct human contact; and in choral music this must always be the case. With me the choirs never use music, which has the double effect: their eyes are not fixed on the page in front of them and they can communicate directly with me.

RO And with the audience. I remember an astonishingly impassioned account of the finale of Beethoven's Ninth Symphony televised live from Berlin. For some choral music—the *Missa Solemnis* we were watching on film—you don't use a baton either.

HvK No, I have always preferred to do it this way, though I must say the *Missa Solemnis* is a very difficult work to direct. There are passages where Beethoven makes problems that perhaps he would have avoided if he had been able to hear.

RO It is always fascinating to talk about the craft of conducting but in the end there is a certain mystery about it all. Someone—I think it was Klemperer—said that conducting was no more and no less than the 'power of suggestion'. You must have come across examples of this kind of thing.

HvK I remember being in La Scala, Milan, during the war. *L'amico Fritz* was being performed and Mascagni[14] was there at the rehearsal. During the famous Intermezzo the conductor asked Mascagni if he would take over for a moment. By that time Mascagni was an old and disappointed man. He was ill and lame—and as I am now he had great difficulty in getting to the rostrum. But he finally got there and settled himself down and lifted his baton. And—well, the

---

14 Pietro Mascagni (1863–1945), whose early successes with *Cavalleria rusticana* (1890) and *L'amico Fritz* (1891) were never fully repeated. His political opportunism during the 1930s is chronicled in Harvey Sachs, *Music in Fascist Italy* (London, 1987), 106 ff.

music started and there was suddenly a great explosion of sound that no one could possibly have been prepared for. I shall never forget that moment. It was incredible.

5 · *Sibelius, Richard Strauss, and the Second Viennese School*

RO   What were your first contacts with the music of Sibelius?

HvK   Whilst I was in Aachen the Head of Swedish Radio invited me to Stockholm to conduct the new Radio Orchestra and I was asked if I would do the Sixth Symphony, which was quite new then and very little known. In fact, it wasn't too difficult because that same week the symphony was being prepared by a man called Pergament-Parmet[1] with the Stockholm Philharmonic and I was able to attend his rehearsals.

RO   I know Sibelius is in many ways a very different composer from Bruckner, but I remember you suggesting that there are for you affinities between them.

HvK   There is in both a sense of the elemental. But I have often asked myself what it is that drew me to Sibelius's music and I think it is that he is a composer who cannot really be compared to anyone else. He is in his way like the Erratic Blocks. They are there, they are colossal, they are of another age; and nobody knows how they came there. So it is better not to ask why. This for me is Sibelius. And you *never* come to an end with him. I think it is perhaps also to do with my love of remote places, my love of mountains rather than cities.

RO   At first you seemed to concentrate on the later works, the Fourth Symphony onwards.

HvK   I conducted the First Symphony during the war but the first two symphonies have always been for me a little too close to Tchaikovsky. At that time, of course, any Sibelius was unfashionable, also Bruckner, and even Brahms who some people said was too 'heavy', like a brick! I often conducted Sibelius in half-empty halls after the war in Vienna.

RO   Legge asked you to record the Fifth Symphony in 1951 and you recorded the last four symphonies between then and the summer of

---

1   Simon Parmet, as he was later known, was born in 1897. He was a conductor and author of a study of the Sibelius symphonies, *Sibelius symfonier* (Helsinki, 1955; London, 1959).

1955. According to Legge, Sibelius's response was: 'Karajan is the only conductor who plays what I meant.'

HvK Yes, he told me that, though I never met Sibelius personally. The Fourth Symphony for me is always a milestone, and very difficult. It is one of the few symphonies—like Brahms's Fourth and Mahler's Sixth—that ends in complete disaster. And the Fifth still has a great fascination for me—in particular, how to bring off the very end of the work. I don't mean technically, though that can cause problems. You know when Beecham was conducting it once a trumpeter came in early in one of the big silences: the kind of catastrophe you can do nothing about. Beecham simply waved at him and called out, 'Thank you, sir!' The real problem here, though, is the huge impact each chord must make. I have had in my mind recently the image of a great bridge, how the pillars rise up and sweep down again with an immense force and weight.

RO Your first Berlin recording of the Sibelius Fifth was one of Glenn Gould's favourite records. He said it was for him the perfect realization of Sibelius as a passionate but anti-sensual composer. You knew Gould?[2]

HvK I had the greatest admiration for his music-making, especially his Bach, which has a special feel for tempo and design. I conducted the Bach D minor Concerto for him once; I think that was the only concert we made together.

RO No, you also played the Beethoven C minor Concerto with him in Berlin in 1957. In one of his essays he says how he boasted to Stokowski that he had an engagement with Karajan in Berlin!

HvK Yes, I had forgotten that. I remember meeting him at about 6 o'clock one morning in an airport in the United States. He'd been there all night sleeping on a bench. We talked a lot and made great plans for a concert tour but in the end the dates weren't right. His death was an immense loss to music.

2 Glenn Gould (1932–82), Canadian pianist who from 1964 confined himself to performances for radio and the gramophone. *The Glenn Gould Reader*, ed. Tim Page (London, 1987), reveals a writing talent commensurate with his pianistic genius.

Karajan recording Sibelius's Fifth
Symphony with the Philharmonia
Orchestra in London in 1960

RO He got very excited about quite a lot of your recordings. There's an EMI Tchaikovsky Fourth Symphony which he described as an incomparably fluid act of musical improvisation; the recording of *Le Sacre* which Stravinsky tried to pillory and which Gould thought the most imaginative and, literally, 'inspiring' recording to date; and one of your recordings of Strauss's *Metamorphosen*.[3]

HvK I loved *Metamorphosen* from the moment the score was published. Everything about it up to the last page where Strauss wrote IN MEMORIAM! and we hear the 'Eroica' theme for the last time. You know, it is only when he came to that final page that he realized where the theme came from, so absorbed was he in the process of composition. It was a Sacher commission. But when I played it I thought that in some of the climaxes the original twenty-three strings were too few to make a full effect. So when we came to make the recording in Vienna I asked Strauss through a mutual friend we had at that time if I could use a fuller body of strings in the climaxes. He said to my friend: 'If he's got the strings, let him do it!'[4] I feel the same about Schoenberg's *Verklärte Nacht*; it is a much more effective piece when it is played in the version for orchestral strings.

RO I want to come back to Schoenberg and the Second Viennese School, but Strauss was someone you knew personally?

HvK I knew from an early age his music and his work as a conductor. I met him properly only once. I was conducting *Elektra* in Berlin—I think it was around the time of his 75th birthday—and at the end he came and said to me it was the best performance of the opera he

3   Probably Karajan's 1969 Berlin recording. Karajan made the first ever recording of the work for the gramophone with the strings of the Vienna Philharmonic in the autumn of 1947, first issued on Columbia LX1082-5.

4   Paul Sacher (b. 1906) founded the Basle Chamber Orchestra in 1926, for which he commissioned major works by such composers as Bartók, Hindemith, Honegger, Ibert, Martin, Martinů, Roussel, Richard Strauss, Stravinsky, and Tippett. He also commissioned Hans Werner Henze's *Sonata per archi* (1957-8), a work where, again, Karajan asked permission to perform it with a full complement of strings. The effect, Henze recalls, was overwhelming. He also recalls the extraordinary care Karajan took over the preparation of the Berlin performances in 1959. See Peter Csobádi (ed.), *Karajan oder die kontrollierte Ekstase* (Vienna, 1988), 158-9.

Karajan with Richard Strauss
and Heinz Tietjen, Berlin, 1941

had ever heard. I said, 'I don't really want to hear this; tell me
what was wrong with it.' I think he was surprised by my reaction,
so he asked me to lunch the next day. He said, 'You have made the
music very clear, the *fp* here, the accent there; but these are not at
all important. Just wave your stick around a bit!' He made a
gesture like stirring a pudding. But what he meant was, let the
music flow naturally. And then he added something which made a
deep impression on me. He said, 'I can see you have worked on
this opera for many months and concentrated very hard. You
conduct it without the score in front of you, which I couldn't do
any more as I am far away from the work. So you are right and I
am wrong! But'—and he laughed—'don't forget that in five years'
time you will have changed again.' The great wisdom of an old
man!

RO I am interested by the idea of the tempo that flows naturally.
Strauss had this ability as a conductor?

HvK He had an impeccable sense of rhythm, not in the metronomic,
military sense of the term but in his feel for the real inner rhythm
of the music he was conducting. You see, if a performance lacks
this it becomes boring; and with Strauss you always had the sense
of the music moving forward. In Mozart this was wonderful.

RO Some of his Mozart recordings seem a little dry.

HvK He could be negligent at times, but he was a very undemonstrative
conductor. With him the slightest gesture would produce positive
results. And he showed no emotion when conducting. His
upbeat—you know how with many conductors this is a great
upwards gesture and then a dreadful flop back down—with him
there was none of this. The emotion came through the music. He
knew in each piece exactly where the real climaxes were and he
avoided completely the kind of hurrying or dragging which ruins
so many performances.

RO On the films we have of him conducting, his face is impassive, like
a mask. Was this true of him generally? Some people thought him
very naïve, especially politically.

HvK People said he was a fool, but I think he knew exactly what he was doing. Even when he was very successful as a young man they had made jokes about his music. But then he made his name, and his money. He lived comfortably; he had his family to protect. This appearance of naïvety was a mask; it was his revenge on lesser people than himself. You remember, he was appointed President of the Reichsmusikkammer in 1933 at the time when he was working on *Die schweigsame Frau* with Stefan Zweig. He wanted Zweig to return to Germany to continue working on other projects. When Zweig wouldn't come, Strauss lost his temper and wrote the famous letter attacking all politicians and everyone who lets politics get in the way of art. The Nazis intercepted the letter[5] and he was obliged to resign from the Reichsmusikkammer. But to Strauss the Nazis were a bunch of Hottentots.

RO I'm told your memories of the whole period of the collapse of the old Austro-Hungarian Empire are fascinating. You must have met in real life quite a few Baron Ochses when you were in Salzburg in the 1920s.

HvK To some extent Ochs is a 'type', but it is true there were many Baron Ochses living in Austria between the wars and living in their castles in a style that was far from elegant—in fact, very uncomfortable, as these were not good times for such people. What annoyed me when I saw Ochs on stage in productions at that time was that he was played as a grotesque, everything greatly exaggerated. But Ochs is not a buffoon. He has been at court, he is an educated man. He may have the smell of the countryside about him but he knows how to behave.

RO Like Falstaff?

HvK Like Falstaff. He has his little failings, his women, and so on. In the Third Act he realizes that the world is against him but he is intelligent enough to know that he is the victim of his own weaknesses.

5 Written by Strauss on 17 June 1935. The letter is quoted and further discussed in Norman Del Mar's *Richard Strauss* (London, 1972), iii. 49.

RO You conducted *Elektra* again in Salzburg in 1964—I remember Szell, who also knew Strauss, giving you and your cast long and heartfelt applause at the end of the performance—and a *Salome* was announced for that time, too, which didn't in fact come about for a number of years.

HvK This was because at that time I could not find a Salome. Strauss once bitterly complained to me. He said, 'Nowadays all the heavy voices are singing this role; it's all gone out of control. I *don't* want this!' His ideal at this time was Cebotari.[6]

RO What about Welitsch?[7]

HvK Oh yes, she was an exception; but physically she was not exactly . . . . in any case I had determined never to do *Salome* with a girl who dances. Either the dance will be no good, or if it is that overwhelming, then she has no energy left to sing the final scene.

RO Then in the mid-seventies you discovered Hildegard Behrens.

HvK I went to hear her in Düsseldorf. She was singing on stage when we arrived and by the time I had reached my seat I said to the man who was with me, this is the Salome I have been looking for. She had very much the Cebotari voice, but a much stronger character. She had the technique for the role—she sang up to a high F if necessary and could cope very well with the low undertones Salome has—and she had what is most important: a real erotic appeal in the voice.

RO The production was something of a hit. Bernstein recently said it's the best *Salome* he's ever seen.

HvK I know, but here is a problem. We did not film it and that is

6 Maria Cebotari (1910–49) was widely admired for the freshness and charm of her singing and her stage presence. She created the role of Aminta in Strauss's *Die schweigsame Frau*. Karajan made some 78 r.p.m. recordings with her, including an aria from Johann Strauss's *Der Zigeunerbaron* and Ariadne's 'Es gibt ein Reich'.

7 Ljuba Welitsch (b. 1913) sang Salome for Strauss in 1944 and won a wider audience for her interpretation with a famous recording of the closing scene made with Fritz Reiner and the Metropolitan Opera Orchestra. Ill health and attendant vocal problems dogged her career from the early 1950s onwards.

something which even now makes me feel completely frustrated.[8]
We had Behrens, we had the designs—have you seen the set for the
first performances of *Salome*? They were not good!

RO   Well, I remember you once saying that the Belle Époque—the age
of *Lulu* and Jacques Lartigue—wasn't to your taste! Your
recordings of Strauss's orchestral works have become something of
a legend, including works like the *Sinfonia Domestica* and the
Alpine Symphony, which you have done a great deal to rehabilitate
in public esteem.

HvK   When Deutsche Grammophon asked me to record the *Alpine
Symphony*, I warned them that it would be very expensive. It needs
a very large orchestra and I needed a lot of rehearsals so that I
could have time to explain the piece fully to the orchestra.[9] It is a
piece that shows Strauss's deep understanding of nature, and, again,
it shows him as the great master of the musical epilogue. The
greatest of the epilogues for me comes at the end of *Don Quixote*
where Quixote says, 'I have battled, I have made mistakes, but I
have lived my life as best I can according to the world as I see it,
and now . . .'. I find this intensely moving. It is a work I have to
come back to again and again. Our last recording was with the
cellist António Meneses, which I admired very much because of the
great beauty of line Meneses was able to bring to the epilogue. But
I have recorded it several times: with Fournier, and Rostropovich.
Rostropovich was wonderful. When we started rehearsing, we
arrived at the cello's first entry and he came in with a dreadful slow
grumbling noise. I was so surprised, I stopped the orchestra and
went over to him. I said, 'Slava, are you all right?' He looked at me
and said, 'Yes, but, you see, it's a very old horse that I'm riding.'
Wonderful! When we are rehearsing and recording he never
touches a drop of alcohol; but afterwards there are many toasts and
celebrations. He is a man I like enormously.

8   The performance was, however, recorded and is now available on CD.

9   Recorded in Berlin, December 1980. Karajan's unique attention to detail shows through
not only in the great dramatic peaks and the long epilogue but also in the famous
passage of the Apparition in the Waterfall (the Alpine Witch of Byron's *Manfred*). Even
more astonishing than the iridescence of the Berlin playing is the sense of the numinous
conveyed by the performance at this point.

Karajan with Mstislav Rostropovich
in the Jesus-Christus-Kirche,
Berlin, in 1968

RO Thinking of epilogues, and closed books, and the passing of time, how do you see the Marschallin?

HvK As a woman who is young in years by our own standards but who is thought old by those of her own time. The end of Act I is a recognition scene; a recognition by the Marschallin of the kind we all experience when we realize that something we cherished is gone for ever. It is not tragic. Tragedy is doing something in spite of the conditions. We come to tragedy through personal misjudgement. But the Marschallin does not misjudge, nor does she sentimentalize the situation. She knows exactly what she is doing.

RO And, of course, Strauss also wrote wonderful music as a very old man.

HvK But you can do this—the *Four Last Songs*, *Metamorphosen*, and this beautiful Oboe Concerto. This is why in all great cultures you find a congress of the old. They have great experience and much to tell us.

RO And Mahler? You deliberately delayed conducting his music until you thought the moment ripe. What had you in mind?

HvK This I can answer exactly. I spent three years in Vienna as a student. We heard this music—Mahler, Webern, Schoenberg—a great deal; it was our daily bread. Then the war came and after the war the concert-managers offered me a chance to do all the Mahler symphonies. I asked them, 'How much rehearsal do I get?' 'Two rehearsals for each concert.' I said, 'Gentlemen, please forget it.' Mahler is very difficult for an orchestra. First, you must, as a painter would say, make your palette. But the difficulty is great, and the greatest danger is that if it is not well performed the music can seem banal. I conduct a lot of light music and it can be very difficult for an orchestra to realize it properly. I once spent a whole rehearsal on the Barcarolle from *Les Contes d'Hoffmann*, which is for me one of the most tragic things in opera. It is not joyful; a man goes from life to death. And in Mahler there is much of this. When we prepared the Fifth Symphony,[10] we recorded it as a trial,

10 During 1972, with a recording in Berlin in February 1973.

worked on it again, then recorded it properly—sixty hours before we first gave it in public!

RO   I remember the concert performances you gave in Berlin in December 1977. They had an extraordinary tension and were in some ways quite different from the earlier recording.

HvK   I remember, and I also remember that it is a very tiring work. By the time you reach the end you have forgotten in what age you began it! After the first two movements, after such great torture, all you can do is let the music flow. But, then, the most difficult movement to play is the third. It needs great skill.

RO   Do you see in the first two movements of the Fifth and in the whole of the Sixth a certain prophetic note, or do you see them in purely musical terms?

HvK   The collapse of a culture and the foresight of everything that was coming is here, certainly. But it has always been the privilege of the genius to know these things before other men.

RO   The great Mahler conductors of an earlier generation, Bruno Walter, for instance, conducted his music very obviously from within the Austro-Hungarian tradition, with a sense of nostalgia, decay, and incipient tragedy. Your Mahler performances have always seemed to carry a starker, more purely tragic message.

HvK   The Sixth is for me one of the greatest symphonies—and so seldom played in the past! There we have complete catastrophe. It is there in the Ninth but in the Ninth there is great beauty and a sense of harmony with death. Coming to the end of this symphony is one of the hardest tasks in all conducting.

RO   Your work on the Ninth was spread across nearly four years. First the LP recording, then the 1982 concert performances, and finally the live Berlin recording for CD in September 1982.

HvK   With the CD we had the feeling that if there was no noise in the hall we could have an even better result. And I know I was madly, madly involved with the symphony to the extent that when it was

OSTER FESTSPIELE SALZBURG 1982

ORCHESTERKONZERT

Montag, 5. April · 18.30 Uhr
Samstag, 10. April · 18.30 Uhr

Großes Festspielhaus

ORCHESTERKONZERT

BERLINER PHILHARMONISCHES ORCHESTER

Dirigent
HERBERT VON KARAJAN

GUSTAV MAHLER

SYMPHONIE NR. 9 D-DUR

Andante comodo
Im Tempo eines gemächlichen Ländlers, etwas täppisch und sehr keck
Rondo — Burleske (Allegro assai, sehr trotzig)
Adagio (sehr langsam und noch zurückhaltend)

done—and it is one of the few works I say this of—I would not dare touch it again.

RO I remember the performance at the 1982 Salzburg Easter Festival. We had booked a table for dinner after the concert—you begin your festival concerts early when we can still concentrate on the music!—and we had to cancel it, we couldn't eat.

HvK I know, it was the same with me. This kind of thing happens once in a lifetime.

RO You have mentioned the problems Webern had with poor performances in the 1930s. Your own four-record set devoted to music of the Second Viennese School was, I know, one of your most cherished projects.[11]

HvK No one wanted me to do the set, so I paid for it myself. And, you know, I worked out that if you pile up all the sets—the record and cassette boxes—we eventually sold, they would reach to the top of the Eiffel Tower. This, I must say, gave me great pleasure.

RO You made special use of recording technology for this set, especially in the Schoenberg Variations, Op. 31.

HvK I began the project with the orchestra several years before we made the recordings. We spent a great deal of time familiarizing ourselves with the music by playing it at subscription concerts and youth concerts. But I knew from the outset that the demands Schoenberg makes in these Variations are abnormal ones which are difficult to realize properly, even in acoustically suitable concert-halls. For the recording, we reseated the orchestra for each variation to create the acoustic that one sees and imagines when one looks at the score. Some people said this was 'manipulation' of the music by technology; but it is the very reverse. When Schoenberg asks for the piccolo to play *ppp* in the top level of its register 'so schwach

11 The Deutsche Grammophon set, recorded between 1972 and 1974 and first issued in 1975, included: Berg, *Three Orchestral Pieces*, Op. 6, three pieces from the *Lyric Suite*; Schoenberg, *Verklärte Nacht*, Op. 4, *Pelléas und Mélisande*, Op. 5, Variations for Orchestra, Op. 31; Webern, Passacaglia for Orchestra, Op. 1, Five Movements, Op. 5, Six Pieces for Orchestra, Op. 6, and the Symphony, Op. 21. All of it is now on CD.

wie möglich'[12] with the bassoon and solo strings at different
dynamic levels, and then asks for completely different textures and
dynamics in the next variation, I know that this cannot be properly
realized by an orchestra in a concert-hall seated in the conventional
way. Realizing the Schoenberg Variations was technically the most
fascinating thing in the set.[13]

RO   You drafted your own advertisement—manifesto almost—for the
set. This touched on several important aesthetic issues, including
the question of whether a musical sound can ever legitimately be
ugly in itself.

HvK   I said to the orchestra, 'If there are discords we must always play
them as beautifully as we know how.' A discord is not an excuse
for ugly music-making, for playing out of tune.[14]

---

12   'As weakly as possible'. Karajan is referring here to var. VII.

13   Peter Stadlen, who began his career as a leading proponent of the music of the Second
Viennese School, wrote in the *Daily Telegraph* on 27 January 1975: 'Karajan's
performance of Schoenberg's Orchestral Variations, Op. 31 proves that it was not mere
eccentricity if he insisted, during recording sessions, on re-seating his players for each
variation. The work gains considerably in plausibility not only through unprecedented
clarity but though a creative acoustical logic.'

14   In the text Karajan drafted for the advertisement, he is even more explicit: 'At our many
rehearsals I repeated this again and again: "Gentlemen, a dissonance is a tension and a
consonance is therefore the necessary and corresponding relaxation. But neither of them,
tension or relaxation, can be ugly, because then they no longer constitute music any
more." I have in mind this nonsense, which one is always hearing, that I want to
"smooth of the rough edges". One can only smooth off rough edges where the
roughness consists of a note being played unprofessionally, i.e. when it is unclean,
untidy, and unattractive. In our work together we have often rehearsed the intonation
for hours on end. The tension too should be a thing of beauty. The musical content
must be clean and pure. Webern is an example of this. It is frequently asserted that he
was very cold. Yet I've often seen him conducting, and I didn't find him so cold at all,
on the contrary: his commitment was immense. Perhaps, though, one point should be
mentioned: in his later years he became much more abstract, more introvert. The
Passacaglia, his Op. 1, which is also included in this set, is a musical work of great
passion. I see no reason for performing it as anything else. The works appear in the
order in which they were composed. We first meet Webern with the Passacaglia and
leave him with the Symphony. What a contrast! Webern's Symphony is a work which I
first came to understand during the rehearsals. I must admit that it is only now that I
know what it is about. It is a kind of abstract music that offers no development, but a
condition, and in fact a condition which remains constant. I cannot tell you how much
this work fascinates me.'

Dmitry Shostakovich with Karajan
and the Berlin Philharmonic after
a performance of Shostakovich's
Tenth Symphony in Moscow
Conservatory in 1969

RO   Mozart once said, 'Passions, whether violent or not, must never be expressed in such a way as to excite disgust.' But you were obviously excited by the content of the music in this set, in the Schoenberg Variations, the Webern Symphony.

HvK   Yes, but in the end it is always the Berg *Three Orchestral Pieces* that moves me most. It is a tremendously difficult work. He wrote it just before the start of the Great War. To conduct it is a devastating experience: it takes up all your mind and it will take you two or three days to recover from it.

RO   You were six years old when the First World War began; later you were to live through some of the worst days of the blitz in Berlin. Perhaps it's no coincidence that some of your readings that have made the most indelible impression on your audiences have been of works like the Berg *Three Orchestral Pieces*, the Honegger *Liturgique*. I also sense that the Shostakovich Tenth Symphony has meant a great deal to you.

HvK   One of the most beautiful experiences of my life was being able to play the Tenth Symphony for Shostakovich when we last visited Moscow. I must say, the orchestra on this occasion was marvellous. I remember Shostakovich was so nervous but at the same time so impressed. He said, 'I can't speak, but . . .'.

RO   What can an interpreter hope to achieve, playing a symphony before the man who wrote it?

HvK   In this case it was to play the symphony as Shostakovich might have imagined it in his dreams.

RO   You have played far more contemporary music over the years than most people care to remember: a lot of Henze at one time, and more recently music through to Ligeti and Penderecki.

HvK   Yes, but I can only do it if I am convinced. It is very easy sometimes but with other works it is difficult if you get a score and you don't know what the composer is thinking. In such cases it is better not to do it than to do it badly. One thing is very probable, though, and that is that the next generation will have no problems in understanding the music of today. The human mind does not adapt very quickly to these changes in style, but if the thing is carefully prepared then eventually it will be understood. I remember when a work like Bartók's *Music for Strings, Percussion, and Celeste* was thought quite impossible, and we now play it like a Concerto Grosso of Handel! When we made our second Berlin recording[15] we recorded the piece, which lasts 31 minutes, in no more than 40 minutes. The players could have played it without a conductor, we knew it so well at that time. But with all these things I prepared and waited, prepared and waited until I had the orchestra really in hand.

RO   Where they exist, would you study a composer's own recordings—Stravinsky's, for instance?

HvK   Of course, but there is always the problem of deciding how successful Stravinsky the conductor has been in realizing his own score.

RO   'The rhythms must be treated organically, not metronomically', I remember you once saying of *Le Sacre*. You've wanted for a long time to conduct *Le Sacre* in the theatre?

HvK   Yes, I wanted to do a production with Balanchine,[16] but it never happened, and now there is no one I can think I would want to do it with.

RO   When did you meet Balanchine? Was it in the 1930s after he had left the Diaghilev company?

HvK   No, it was much later than that. I knew his work, of course. He created *Apollo*, which I have conducted a great deal. I was enormously impressed by his staging of Stravinsky's *Agon*. He had a genius for staging that was absolutely simple; and he knew

15   Berlin, 1969, for Deutsche Grammophon. Karajan made a very successful EMI recording of the work with the Berlin Philharmonic in 1960 and an earlier one for EMI with the Philharmonia Orchestra in 1949.

16   George Balanchine (1904–83) was trained at the Imperial Ballet School, St Petersburg, and left Russia to join Diaghilev's Ballets Russes in 1924. Choreography for Stravinsky's *Apollon musagète*, Paris, 1928. Director of the New York City Ballet from 1948.

music—ballet, the symphonic repertoire—as well as any conductor. This combination of simplicity and real musical knowledge was something very special for me.

RO And you worked with Jean Cocteau on *Oedipus rex*.

HvK He came to Vienna for our performances of *Oedipus rex*; he was the Narrator. He was a unique person with a fascinating understanding of the arts in all their forms. I collected him from the airport and he scarcely drew breath! Yet everything he talked of was clear and at the tip of his tongue. I plan to do *Oedipus* again, not staged, but in concert with certain lighting effects.

RO I remember suggesting that you might do Bellini's *Norma* that way.

HvK Perhaps it could be done as an oratorio. I would never do it in the theatre; I have seen it and—well, the people are just there to hear the singers. There was a possibility that we might record it some years ago—such great music, no wonder Wagner was overwhelmed by it!

RO One final twentieth-century composer: William Walton. He became a great fan of yours after a particularly exciting performance you conducted of *Belshazzar's Feast*.

HvK I liked him very much. I remember he rang me once—he could be very amusing—and said, 'I am writing a Theme and Variations. I've written the Variations but I don't yet have the Theme'![17] He was a wonderful man.

17 Possibly the *Varii Capricci* of 1976, the year Karajan declined to conduct a projected commission from the Greater London Council, *Adagio ed Allegro Festivo*. Walton's admiration for Karajan, who conducted the First Symphony as well as *Belshazzar's Feast* in the 1950's, turned to bitterness ('he's the most dreadful shit') when the older Karajan ceased to play his music (see Michael Kennedy, *Portrait of Walton*, Oxford 1989, p. 263).

6 · Gramophone and Film: The Recorded Legacy

RO　You began your recording career in Berlin in 1938 with the Staatskapelle and a performance of the Overture to *Die Zauberflöte*. The age of gaslight, I think you called it.

HvK　Yes, it wasn't always very easy making ten-inch 78 r.p.m. records— four minutes each side—often with planes flying overhead from the nearby airport. We also lost many recordings: the wax masters could be broken. I remember once a whole plane-load getting delayed and when they were unpacked the frost had cracked most of them.

RO　Your recording career began in earnest in 1946 with Legge in Vienna. What strikes me about it is not only the great repertory you've covered and the astonishing sales figures that must now be in the region of a hundred million, but the creative way you've used the medium in conjunction with your years of work with the Berlin Philharmonic. When we first met, you were making your second Berlin cycle of the nine Beethoven symphonies.

HvK　You see, normally when a recording is made, the symphony is played, rehearsed, recorded, and then it's finished. What I was able to do in that instance was play all the symphonies through with the orchestra and then forget about them for three months. And then we came back to them, one after the other, and said, 'Now, where does this take us?' And there you can begin to see the faults. But it takes time, time, time. On the first occasion something will go well, but maybe after a time you will see that it was not right. And from then on we started the *real* work and the real recording. Then after half a year we get the tapes and they go back and we say that something may have to be changed. I remember we made a completely new recording of the 'Funeral March' of the 'Eroica' Symphony because I felt it was not the right tempo. When you spread work like this over a very long period you are able to look into yourself, and see yourself in a great work of art. Taking the score out of my brief-case and putting it on the podium: that is not my way.

RO　Does a recording exist in a different dimension of time from a live performance?

Akio Morita, President of Sony,
with Karajan at the first public
presentation of the compact disc,
Salzburg, Easter 1981

HvK   A different dimension of time: no. It was a nonsense they tried to teach me when I first made records, you must always do it faster. For me it is always the same, though we now have the added good fortune of playing live concerts and recording in the Philharmonie. This, too, has made an enormous difference—no longer having to work in a studio.

RO   Yet in something like the Schoenberg Op. 31 Orchestral Variations you used the recording process in a quite radical way?

HvK   There I had the idea of the kind of sound you could never have in the concert-hall, a sound that exists only in the imagination and in the new kind of acoustic reality we were able to create through the recording itself.

RO   As in all things, you have a team which has been with you for many years?

HvK   Hermanns[1] has been with me for over twenty years; he is the best recording engineer I know. And Glotz[2] has for many years now supervised all my recordings. I trust his judgement completely. His ear is like my own, and he is very good with the crew. He keeps up their morale and always remembers to see that they are thanked properly. He is always giving people small presents! He has the responsibility for all the editing.

RO   And there are parallel teams for your film work headed by people like Ernst Wild.

HvK   I have learned what I know *with* them. It is like the crew of a sailing-boat; you build a team and over the years you make your performances together.

RO   I think as early as 1947 you said you must one day make music on film.

1   Günter Hermanns, Karajan's principal recording engineer with Deutsche Grammophon since the early 1960s.

2   Michel Glotz has overseen Karajan's recordings since 1965. Before that he had worked closely with Sir Thomas Beecham and Maria Callas.

HvK   It is part of the explosion of interest in music there has been this
      century. When I was a boy in Salzburg two or three hundred
      people might hear a concert, listening to something that the great
      majority of people outside the concert-hall had no knowledge or
      understanding of. Today music is an international language;
      through records and films and television you can reach audiences of
      millions of people. Bringing music to so many people has been the
      great satisfaction of my life. Music is no longer something only for
      those who have the knowledge or the money. That audience still
      exists but we can also reach out beyond it.

RO   True, but how, and at what level of artistic achievement? I saw a
      live TV transmission of *Il trovatore* from the Metropolitan in New
      York a few weeks ago[3] that can only have confirmed a lot of
      people's worst prejudices about opera—dull production, dull
      filming, all wrapped round with a certain amount of superstar
      hype.

HvK   I know, we had it here, too. My response to these people is, if you
      can't do the thing properly, then, please, do not do it at all. And
      here I must agree that I am beginning to fear that we may be on
      the edge of an age of the worst kind of mass production. Before
      long if we are not careful we shall be overwhelmed with things that
      are tenth-rate.

RO   People think that because you have sold millions of records and are
      now also in films that you are part of this movement; which is why
      it would be helpful to discuss in a little detail what your work
      really involves. Your serious working on filming music goes back
      to the 1960s?

HvK   For over twenty years I have been experimenting with how we
      show music: not only the work of the orchestra, how they play,
      but also the way the instruments are brought in as part of the
      musical argument. One or two of the old films are now on CD
      video[4] because they are important documents of certain artists, but

3   On 15 October 1988.
4   R. Strauss's *Don Quixote* with Rostropovich, and some opera sets.

the way we are filming and editing the films I am now making is completely different. We have learnt a very great deal in these years, and so we forget about the older films, just as you wouldn't dream of driving around in a thirty-year-old car.

RO   Did you learn anything about yourself when watching your early films?

HvK   Of course. People will tell you how something may not be quite right. But it is when one sees it for oneself that the problem is really understood.

RO   Film threatens to alter our image of the conductor. Traditionally, he has been rather a mysterious figure with most of the audience seeing only his back. In fact, Elias Canetti once suggested that if the conductor were to turn fully round during a performance the spell he exerts would be broken.[5]

HvK   Our experience with the Philharmonie suggests that this isn't true. In this hall we have good sound in all the seats, including those that look towards the conductor. When we opened the hall, most of the subscribers wanted to sit facing the conductor because from there they were able to follow all the developments of the performance much better.

RO   But in the hall they can see everything. So many television transmissions, and some of these are now on CD video, provide endless, often arbitrary, shots of the conductor at the expense of the musical developments going on around him. There's a Bruckner CD video where at one point the conductor is filmed doing absolutely nothing, whilst the orchestra is busy starting up a new paragraph of the music.

HvK   Yes, I have seen this kind of thing and it is something we avoid completely. In my films the conductor is more or less in one position throughout. But, you see, we have the resources to create an image not just of the conductor or the orchestra but of the whole ensemble of the music and the performers. First of all, we

5   Elias Canetti, *Crowds and Power* (London, 1973), 458–60.

have three banks of cameras: left, right, and diagonally. And there are five cameras in each group. At the start of the filming we bring in a students' orchestra and we rehearse for three days, six sessions in all. And during this time I am on the monitor studying the whole thing so that we can make our plans and adjustments for our filming with the real orchestra. In my mind the whole time there is the simple question, 'What is it the music is supposed to say?' Because we have so many cameras I can have for the editing a great many possibilities; and if we have filmed the music properly in the first place we can already have created some very important effects just with one shot—the violins may have the principal melody with an important counter-melody or harmonic detail in the violas, so we might shoot the passage in such a way that we have the violin bows in the foreground, the conductor, and the violas clearly focused as the third element in the shot.

RO   There are no doubt directors who claim—whatever the reality—that they are doing this kind of thing already, albeit with less lavish resources. What they don't have is the conductor's ear and conductor's-eye view of the music.

HvK   When I conduct a symphony or make a film, I have the impression of the complete work in my mind. This is not with me a photographic thing. My great friend Mitropoulos[6] had a photographic memory; the players would watch him and say, 'Now he turns the page!' With me it is the sound of groups of bars that form a phrase. But, certainly, it is my aim to show the work as it is constructed, the ebb and flow of the tension, the musical line, the many voices, and so on.

RO   I don't think this point has been properly understood by many people who have been given the impression that the films are a kind of expensive toy, when in fact you are the first conductor in history to use film as an integral extension of your work as an interpretative artist.

6   Dimitri Mitropoulos (1896–1960), Greek conductor, pianist, and composer. One of the most charismatic conductors of the century, with an ability to run rehearsals, including rehearsals of new contemporary music, from memory. A formative influence on Leonard Bernstein. Frequent appearances at post-war Salzburg Festivals.

HvK   To make an image of the music that will deepen the understanding of those who watch. I remember some years ago being called by a man who told me he had just now heard things for the first time in the Beethoven Fifth. I said, 'This is very good, but the performance you are talking of is on film. Don't you mean "seen"?' 'No, I mean *heard*.' This is the power of film when it is properly used.

RO   Watching the editing of the Brahms Second Symphony I must say I forgot I was watching a film, simply because I was fascinated to hear new colours which the eye was suggesting by the way you were using shots of the violas and the trombones at some of the quietest moments in the work.

HvK   The ideal must be when the picture and the sound make a complete agreement. I remember having an extraordinary experience watching the film of *Apocalypse Now*. The famous sequence when the helicopters gather in the sky before the great attack has music with it—very familiar music!—but, do you know, I was so gripped by the power of Coppola's image, the helicopters, the music, that it wasn't until many, many hours afterwards that I realized what the music was he had been using.[7]

RO   You also value immediacy, none of those vague middle-distance shots we get in some concert transmissions.

HvK   The limit is four or five metres. Perhaps once in a film, for a special moment, I might show the whole orchestra, or perhaps at the very end, with the lights down. But as a general rule the image must be at no more than five metres distance.

RO   Clearly, after your rehearsal sessions, and with fifteen cameras at your disposal, you can avoid the problems you often get with live concerts. You can adapt the lighting, for instance.

HvK   Certainly. And this is important because a man might look very well from one side but he might look like a cheese from another, and that would be a distraction.

7   'The Ride of the Valkyries'. If Karajan did not recognize the music at the time it is an extraordinary tribute to Coppola's skills.

Karajan directing a filmed
orchestral performance in 1968

RO   Again, contrary to some reports I've seen in newspapers, you don't film only instruments, to the exclusion of the players' faces.

HvK   Naturally, it depends what is appropriate to the music. Sometimes we can get a good impression of the player but it might be necessary to take some more shots later in the studio.[8] At other times we will focus only on the instruments, and here you can make effects that are almost abstract. In Smetana's 'Moldau',[9] in the night sequence it is possible to use the lights and the textures of the instruments to create a night-time, moonlit effect. It must not be overdone, but it can make a suggestion of mood that the listener will have.

RO   Almost subliminal.

HvK   Well, this is interesting. How brief can a shot be? You know, in some countries it is against the law to put into advertisements shots that are shorter than so many parts of a second. Otherwise it becomes brain-washing. But I can do what I want, so perhaps it is possible to use one or two frames of a timpani shot to realize a particular moment in the music.

RO   Filming orchestral music is obviously an art which you've given special thought to and you are pioneering your own editing methods in the light of your long musical and interpretative experience. Some of your Salzburg opera productions are also going on film, too?

HvK   Yes. We don't have everything by any means; and as I have already said, I bitterly regret not having our *Salome*. In opera we are also learning all the time. Some of the older films—the *Don Giovanni*,[10] for instance—were interesting but they were badly edited. You hear Zerlina singing and it sounds as though her voice is coming not out of her mouth but out of a tree on the other side of the set.

---

8   Karajan has spent a great deal of time and money on this. The sound-track is unaltered but a passage may be reshot to allow for adjustments to lighting in, say, the violin solo in the Benedictus of Beethoven's *Missa Solemnis*, or for the player in something like the tuba solos in Strauss's *Don Quixote* to take on a more rubicund appearance.

9   *Má vlast*, No. 2, 'Vltava'.

10   Directed by Joseph Losey, 1979.

RO What about the troublesome matter of subtitles and the encoding of multilingual versions on to the CD videos?

HvK I have nothing to do with that. I will not allow subtitles on my films. This is home video, and if the person is not familiar with the text, then it is possible perhaps to have a libretto and translation to one side. But I will never allow subtitles on the film itself.[11]

RO It is important to stress that home video is not videotape but CD video with a high-quality television monitor and high-quality digital sound played through adjacent high-fidelity speakers.

HvK And for this reason we are looking for a suitable name. The company is called Télémondial but this is nothing to do with television or ordinary video. So we are looking for a new name that we shall use for the discs when they are eventually released.

RO You have over DM 50 million tied up in the project but you are very patient about the eventual time of launch.

HvK The main thing is that we have now completed over forty films. When I started six years ago I didn't know, shall I still be living when this project is completed? I am free of that worry now. We have completed a great deal and the team knows exactly how a thing must be done, so it is simply a question of completing the sequence, designing our record packaging, and also seeing how the market is developing for the video players and monitors. We have also to be very careful about copyright. The old videotapes lost a great deal of money because they were immediately taken and sold in pirate copies.

RO I think it was Stokowski in the early 1930s who first became seriously interested in filming music as you have done, but he never got anywhere with it. He was born too early!

HvK But if I am honest I would like to have been born perhaps six or seven years later. I think there will be great developments over the next few years. But I have made the films as I wanted them. I hope

11 Nor 'surtitles' in the theatre. Karajan, who said he had never heard of such a thing, greeted my explanation with disbelief.

people will want to see them. But if they don't—well, they are there as a record.

RO   I can't imagine for a moment that they will be sitting unwatched in some archive. But their archive value is also important.

HvK   We have no film of Nikisch[12]—imagine the fascination of that if we had. I would give my right arm for just thirty seconds. I remember after the war in Bayreuth spending many hours with an old bass player who had worked under him. He told me many things that were deeply fascinating. I am also happy that we shall have a record of the Berlin orchestra. The many hours we have spent playing, seeing, hearing whilst making these films have taught us a great deal. Watching ourselves teaches us much about how we perform.

RO   Have the films brought about improvements even for that great orchestra?

HvK   Yes, I think so. And I like to think in fifty or a hundred years' time it will not be possible for any orchestra to play sloppily and claim that it is not possible to do better. It is a great joy for me to see the discipline and enthusiasm of these players. It is something that is very special, and their example is now preserved for future generations of musicians to study and enjoy.

12   Arthur Nikisch (1855–1922), principal conductor of the Berlin Philharmonic from 1895 to 1922, and from his début in Leipzig in 1879 one of the most remarkable conductors of his age. Tchaikovsky wrote of him as being 'elegantly calm, sparing of superfluous movements, yet at the same time wonderfully strong and self-possessed. He does not seem to conduct, but rather exercise some mysterious spell . . .'. His influence on conductors as different as Wilhelm Furtwängler and Sir Adrian Boult was profound.

7 · Afterwords

RO You have long considered music to be a therapeutic force in modern society.

HvK In all societies. Read the old sagas and there you will see it is thought of as a great living force.

RO Where do you personally feel it touching the society in which we live?

HvK At many points: social and even ethical as well as aesthetic. First of all, an orchestra, if it is functioning in the best way, is a creative unit. A group of men and women are coming together to re-create something that is beautiful, more beautiful than I can ever realize by simply reading the score. And, again, if it is functioning well, it is possible to see this reflected in the bearing and in the expressions of the players whilst they are making music. This is another aspect of my work with film that has so fascinated me: the physiognomy of a great orchestra when the players are really concentrating, really absorbed in the process of music-making. I have often said to the orchestra, especially to the younger players, 'Do your best, and love what you are doing, because you are allowed to do this thing.' By this I mean, they can do what millions of people cannot do. Many people cannot think of playing music or listening to it until six o'clock in the evening. To be involved professionally in a thing as creative as this is a great privilege and we have a duty to make it in such a way that we can help bring pleasure and a sense of fulfilment to those who are not so fortunate.

RO Music has the great advantage of crossing the normal linguistic barriers.

HvK It unites nations as well as individuals. Today I wake up and what is there but more news of people killing one another?[1]—it is folly but we must do everything in our power to help bring about co-operation between peoples. I admire what Gorbachev is attempting, but I am afraid he has great problems. For one thing, they haven't a proper infrastructure. Even if they can produce more food, they haven't the transport or the packaging facilities. I remember being

1   5 December 1988. Karajan was referring to the racial disturbances in Azerbaijan.

Karajan applauding the orchestra
after a Salzburg Festival
performance

given some caviar once when we were in Russia—wrapped in newspaper because they had no containers to put it in!

RO Someone once said that you weren't much interested in politics except of the musical variety, of which you are a consummate master; but you have been friendly with a number of leading politicians, including two British Prime Ministers.

HvK I have met Edward Heath and also Margaret Thatcher.

RO I don't know how the British press sees Austrian politics but there was a short note in the *Daily Telegraph* announcing that Margaret Thatcher was due to meet the Austrian President and you, with the headline 'Thatcher to meet von Karajan'!

HvK She came to Salzburg to the festival but refused to let anyone put themselves out for her; I was enormously impressed by how kind and unassuming she was. She came to my home for lunch. She said she envied me my position, where people always did what I requested. I had to say that this was not always the case! I have admired her greatly as someone who has an absolutely clear sense of what it is she is trying to achieve.

RO She is, like you, a workaholic.

HvK I must say I have never spared myself, and never will as long as I live. I live simply. I don't smoke. I occasionally have a whisky.

RO You have enjoyed two long marriages. With Eliette von Karajan it has been thirty years of family life, with two daughters, Isabel and Arabel. When did you meet Eliette?

HvK First in Saint Tropez. Then she came to London and I saw her sitting in the twelfth or thirteenth row of the Royal Festival Hall. It was quite a shock!

RO For her too. She told me that the previous year she had confided to an American friend in Rome that the two people who most fascinated her in the world were Albert Schweitzer and Herbert von Karajan; and a year later she was sitting in an empty hall with Walter Legge, Elisabeth Schwarzkopf, and Herbert von Karajan

Karajan and his wife, Eliette

listening to a private recital on the organ by Albert Schweitzer. As well as looking after your daughters and your home, she has also become a painter.

HvK   This is a remarkable thing. She always had an interest in the arts, but in painting she is self-taught. For many years her models were the painters of her native France, and as we spent time in Provence this was a wonderful place for her to work. But now she has gone beyond that. There is the possibility of a major exhibition in Japan and here in our Salzburg house I have made for her a gallery on the second floor.

RO   Well, she said it wasn't quite ready for inspection, but I have seen some work that is in progress that is now very much in her own style: some night forest scenes that are very striking, one very calm, two very anguished.

HvK   She works very hard. But she also spends a great deal of time walking and studying, in the day, at night. She goes off to the city for a few days, but then she is back. Her real love is nature: plants, animals, everything to do with it.

RO   Being the wife of Herbert von Karajan is probably as much a hindrance as a help where some other painters and critics are concerned.

HvK   I think we can have too much of the critics! In Vienna recently there was a really fascinating exhibition. I could not go to it but they showed it on television. And the television was a disaster. Here was a marvellous chance for us to see the paintings but all we had was talk, talk, and more talk about what the paintings were supposed to mean.

RO   And what about the daughters of Herbert von Karajan?

HvK   It has been a great joy to me that we have remained a very close family. We have never had the problem of the children detaching themselves from us. They have their careers, of course. Isabel is an actress now in Vienna and Arabel is studying music in Boston. We were lucky in their schooling. They went to school in Switzerland, which is where our real home is. They had wonderful opportunities for sport and also for learning as many things as possible that might be of use for their future development. But I said, I will take all this from you if I hear that you are playing at being the important person. At the end of one term, one of them said she had a new friend called Lisa. 'Lisa who?' I asked. 'I don't know her surname.' I knew then it was all right. You judge people not by who they are but by what they do and how they behave.

RO They must have heard a lot of wonderful music-making. Arabel was once quoted as being terrified by a performance of Tchaikovsky's *Pathétique* Symphony in Berlin so intense that she thought it would kill you. But she now takes up music rather late in her education.

HvK Well, I think at first they were both afraid to become music specialists, but she knows so much now—good contemporary pop music, not just my music—that she wants to be involved with it and she refuses to be professionally involved unless she has expert knowledge. So, though it is too late to learn the violin or the piano, now we have the very complex musical skills of mixing, using synthesizers; and this she is learning as part of her musical education in Boston.

RO Your family has obviously sustained you through many crises. Looking back at your career to, say, the last years of the Great War I am reminded of that poem quoted at the end of Pasternak's *Dr Zhivago*, 'To live one's life is not as easy as crossing a ploughed field'! The spinal injuries and illnesses, for example.

HvK When that finally came to a crisis I was within four days of complete paralysis. I have not been kind to my back; I had accidents when I was a boy, tree-climbing and biking, and I have spent many years skiing. The disc that slipped had done so in such a way as to be digging into my spinal chord. It had compressed two-thirds of the marrow and trapped the nerves. They took five hours to get it out; and there was a man in the next room who was not so lucky as I was. It happened at Christmas 1975 and the surgeon was just about to leave for a holiday with his family in the Middle

East. He was on his way to the airport when he received a message that I was very ill. He immediately turned round and came back. After an experience like that, each new day you are granted has a special meaning.

RO   Did you ever contemplate becoming a doctor?

HvK   No. My brother and I used to have a joke—we saw how hard our father worked—that we would only consider medicine if we could become specialists in venereal diseases, because we would never have to get up in the middle of the night and we would never be out of work.

RO   Your brother was sixteen months older than you, and a great spur to your competitive instincts.

HvK   I did not see why he should have piano lessons when I was told I was too young; so I hid behind the curtains and listened to what he was being taught. I soon knew so much they could not deny me any longer!

RO   He died, I gather, in 1987.

HvK   Yes, and I don't think it was necessary. He refused to go near a doctor. He had some minor heart ailment, and then a kidney problem which could probably have been treated. But he was always a law to himself. He would go off into the mountains for days on end. No one would know where he was.

RO   He had considerable talent as an electronic engineer, as well as in music?

HvK   He made a radio receiver when we were children and set it up on the main bridge over the Salzach. So many people wanted to see it, the police had to be called to disperse the crowd and take the equipment away. Siemens offered him a studio exclusively for his own private use and research; but he wouldn't take it. One thing I used to wish he would invent: something I could wear round my head—a kind of miner's lamp—that would destroy film in the cameras of people who come to my concerts and take flash photos during the performance.

RO   There was a man behind the orchestra in the Philharmonie who all but ruined what was a fascinating performance of the Fifth Symphony of Beethoven.[2]

HvK   I know. But what can I do? If you throw them out it causes a disturbance.

RO   I admire your restraint! But you also show great restraint over a lot of the stuff that's written about you in the press, a lot of which is ill-informed gossip.

HvK   I can see no point in reacting to it. When I was younger I was often upset by criticism and innuendo but I learnt that if you become involved with this kind of thing it will end up by gnawing you away. I try to keep a certain distance, a certain seclusion. My interest in yoga and the ways of the great Buddhist teachers has helped me a little in this respect. And here again we have a case of the value of the therapeutic power of music itself. Just as it is important to find the right pulse for a piece of music, so you must find the right rhythm by which to live your life. I remember once, I was rehearsing a piece of Bach—I forget which piece it was—and I suddenly felt in a state of absolute harmony. So much so that I stopped the rehearsal at that point.

RO   I remember researching the notes for the Bach Brandenburg Concerto you played when you brought the Berlin Philharmonic to play in the Sheldonian in Oxford and coming across a passage in the writing of that great American philosopher Susanne Langer, where she defines the competent artist as someone whose mind is trained and predisposed to see every option in relation to others and the whole.

HvK   Which is what we mean when we talk of true harmony. But it is not only an abstract thing. I remember my father saying when he was a very old man, 'Technique you can learn. But what comes out

2   Berlin, 4 December 1988.

'When Karajan did Bach', a harpsichordist told H. C. Robbins Landon, 'he shed all virtuoso glamour and made music, and what marvellous music-making it was!'

of it is what you give as a human being. Never forget that you do not operate on a dead thing. You operate on a living body.' He spoke as a doctor but his words left a deep impression on my musical life.

8 · *Epilogue*

*Extract from a conversation at Karajan's home
near Salzburg, March 1988*

RO On 1 January 1987 you conducted the New Year's Day Concert in
Vienna. It is always such a wonderful event, a kind of message of
hope at the start of the year. Was that a special occasion for you?

HvK It was a special occasion. It was a turning-point in my career.

RO A turning-point?

HvK Because I was very much in pain. Sometimes for nights on end I
had no sleep. It was a really hard time. When I got the invitation, I
said 'Well, gladly I will accept.' For three weeks I had nothing to
do and I sat down and decided—I have recorded all these pieces
before—to see if there was not something more behind the music.
So for three weeks, six hours a day, I played the music. And
suddenly I was changed in myself. When I came before the
orchestra, I had nothing to explain. It was just there. And from this
time I knew I had to give up so many things—my sailing and so
on—but the music came back to me a hundred times better.

RO But music has sustained you throughout your life. And you say the
pain went, too?

HvK Yes, I still have difficulty walking, but it went.

RO People say that when you are on the rostrum and start making
music . . .

HvK Yes, I know. It makes me completely happy.

Von Karajan and Opera Production

1. Select list of collaborations with theatre or film directors

1938 Berlin Staatsoper. Mozart, *Die Zauberflöte*. Dir. Gustaf Gründgens.

1941 Aachen Stadttheater. Verdi, *Falstaff*. Dir. Walter Felsenstein.

1948 Salzburg Festival, Felsenreitschule. Gluck, *Orfeo ed Euridice*. Dir. Oscar Fritz Schuh.

1951 Bayreuth Festival. Wagner, *Die Meistersinger von Nürnberg*. Dir. Rudolf Hartmann.

1952 Bayreuth Festival. Wagner, *Tristan und Isolde*. Dir. Wieland Wagner.

1958 Salzburg Festival, Felsenreitschule. Verdi, *Don Carlo*. Dir. Gustaf Gründgens.

1960 Salzburg Festival, Grosses Festspielhaus. Strauss, *Der Rosenkavalier*. Dir. Rudolf Hartmann.

1963 La Scala, Milan. Puccini, *La Bohème*. Dir. Franco Zeffirelli.

1964 La Scala, Milan. Verdi, *La traviata*. Dir. Franco Zeffirelli.

1972 Salzburg Festival, Grosses Festspielhaus. Mozart, *Le nozze di Figaro*. Dir. Jean-Pierre Ponnelle.

1973 Salzburg Festival, Grosses Festspielhaus. Mozart, *Die Zauberflöte*. Dir. Giorgio Strehler.

1987 Salzburg Festival, Grosses Festspielhaus. Mozart, *Don Giovanni*. Dir. Michael Hampe.

2. Complete list of opera productions conducted and directed by Karajan

(i) 1940–1966

1940 Aachen Stadttheater. Wagner, *Die Meistersinger von Nürnberg*. Scenery and costumes: Fritz Riedl.

1941 Aachen Stadttheater. Strauss, *Der Rosenkavalier*. Scenery and costumes: Fritz Riedl.

1950 La Scala, Milan. Wagner, *Tannhäuser*. Scenery and costumes: Emil Preetorius.

1951 La Scala, Milan. Mozart, *Don Giovanni*. Scenery and costumes: Wilhelm Reinking.

1952 La Scala, Milan. Beethoven, *Fidelio*. Scenery and costumes: Emil Preetorius.

1952 La Scala, Milan. Strauss, *Der Rosenkavalier*. Scenery and costumes: Robert Kautsky.

1953 La Scala, Milan. Wagner, *Lohengrin*. Scenery and costumes: Emil Preetorius.

1953   La Scala, Milan. Orff, *Carmina Burana, Catulli Carmina, Trionfo di Afrodite*. Scenery and costumes: Josef Fennecker.

1954   La Scala, Milan. Donizetti, *Lucia di Lammermoor*. Scenery: Gianni Ratto. Costumes: Ebe Colciaghi. (Also Vienna Staatsoper, Berlin Stadtische Oper, 1955.)

1954   La Scala, Milan. Mozart, *Le nozze di Figaro*. Scenery and costumes: Wilhelm Reinking.

1955   La Scala, Milan. Bizet, *Carmen*. Scenery and costumes: Ita Maximowna.

1955   La Scala, Milan. Mozart, *Die Zauberflöte*. Scenery and costumes: Emil Preetorius.

1956   La Scala, Milan. Strauss, *Salome*. Scenery and costumes: Ita Maximowna.

1957   La Scala, Milan. Verdi, *Falstaff*. Scenery and costumes: G. Bartolini-Salimbeni. (Also Vienna Staatsoper, Salzburg Festival, 1957.)

1957   Vienna Staatsoper. Wagner, *Die Walküre*. Scenery and costumes: Emil Preetorius.

1957   Vienna Staatsoper. Verdi, *Otello*. Scenery: Wilhelm Reinking. Costumes: Georges Wakhevitch.

1957   Salzburg Festival, Felsenreitschule. Beethoven, *Fidelio*. Scenery and costumes: Helmut Jürgens.

1957   Vienna Staatsoper. Wagner, *Siegfried*. Scenery and costumes: Emil Preetorius.

1958   Vienna Staatsoper. Wagner, *Das Rheingold*. Scenery and costumes: Emil Preetorius.

1959   Vienna Staatsoper. Wagner, *Tristan und Isolde*. Scenery and costumes: Emil Preetorius.

1960   Vienna Staatsoper. Wagner, *Götterdämmerung*. Scenery and costumes: Emil Preetorius.

1961   Vienna Staatsoper. Wagner, *Parsifal*. Scenery and costumes: Heinrich Wendel.

1962   Vienna Staatsoper. Debussy, *Pelléas et Mélisande*. Scenery: Günther Schneider-Siemssen. Costumes: Charlotte Flemming.

1962   Salzburg Festival, Grosses Festspielhaus. Verdi, *Il trovatore*. Scenery: Teo Otto. Costumes: Georges Wakhevitch. (Also Vienna Staatsoper, 1963; revised, Salzburg Easter Festival, 1977, Vienna Staatsoper, 1977.)

1963   Vienna Staatsoper. Wagner, *Tannhäuser*. Scenery and costumes: Heinrich Wendel.

1964   Vienna Staatsoper. Strauss, *Die Frau ohne Schatten*. Scenery: Günther Schneider-Siemssen. Costumes: Ronny Reiter.

1964   Salzburg Festival, Grosses Festspielhaus. Strauss, *Elektra*. Scenery and costumes: Teo Otto.

Set design by Günther Schneider-
Siemssen for the 1982 Salzburg
Easter Festival production of
Wagner's *Der fliegende Holländer*

1965 Salzburg Festival, Grosses Festspielhaus. Mussorgsky, *Boris
Godunov*. Scenery: Günther Schneider-Siemssen. Costumes: Ronny
Reiter.
1966 Salzburg Festival, Grosses Festspielhaus. Bizet, *Carmen*. Scenery:
Teo Otto. Costumes: Georges Wakhevitch.

(ii) Since 1967, all Karajan's opera productions have had their first
performances at the Easter or Summer Salzburg Festivals in the Grosses
Festspielhaus with scenery by Günther Schneider-Siemssen and costumes
by Georges Wakhevitch, assisted in some instances by Magda Gstrein.

1967	Wagner, *Die Walküre*	1975	Verdi, *Don Carlo*
1968	Wagner, *Das Rheingold*	1976	Wagner, *Lohengrin*
1968	Mozart, *Don Giovanni*	1977	Strauss, *Salome*
1969	Wagner, *Siegfried*	1979	Verdi, *Aida*
1970	Wagner, *Götterdämmerung*	1980	Wagner, *Parsifal*
1970	Verdi, *Otello*	1981	Verdi, *Falstaff*
1971	Beethoven, *Fidelio*	1982	Wagner, *Der fliegende*
1972	Wagner, *Tristan und Isolde*		*Holländer*
1974	Wagner, *Die Meistersinger*	1985	Bizet, *Carmen*
	von Nürnberg	1988	Puccini, *Tosca*

Index

About the Author

Richard Osborne is well known in the United Kingdom and abroad as a contributor to *Gramophone*, the world's leading classical record review magazine. He has also written for the London *Times*, *The Independent*, *Times Literary Supplement*, and *Opera*. He is a full-time writer and broadcaster and the presenter of BBC Radio's principal record review program "Saturday Review." His *Rossini* was widely acclaimed for its readability and scholarship.